Car | 8/74

1948 ed.

The Faber Monographs on Pottery and Porcelain

Edited by W. B. Honey

*

GREEK POTTERY

The Faber Monographs on Pottery and Porcelain
Edited by W. B. HONEY

★

★

OTHER TITLES TO FOLLOW

GREEK POTTERY

by
ARTHUR LANE

FABER AND FABER
24 Russell Square
London

First published in mcmxlviii
by Faber and Faber Limited
24 Russell Square London W.C. 1
Printed in Great Britain by
R. MacLehose and Company Limited
The University Press Glasgow
Colour plates printed by
The Fine Art Engravers Limited, Esher

IN MEMORY OF
HUMFRY PAYNE
ΤΟ ΓΑΡ ΓΕΡΑΣ ΕΣΤΙ ΘΑΝΟΝΤΩΝ

FOREWORD

Greek pottery has commonly been excluded from general surveys of European ceramic art, chiefly because the field has been occupied by the Classical archaeologists. The ceramic historians have been apt to take a revenge for this by declaring that the wares in question, whatever the value of the painting they bear, are without much merit as pottery, having been inspired by examples in metal and revealing in their sharp edges and unnaturally smooth finish no sign of their origin in plastic clay.

These charges can of course be seriously maintained only as regards some of the wares of a narrowly-restricted period; they are much less true in the wider field of Greek pottery in general. Even as regards the 'Classical' wares of the sixth and fifth centuries it may be pointed out that much of the black-figure decoration (for example) depends absolutely on the potter's technique known as *sgraffiato* work, which was used also by the medieval Chinese and Persian potters, amongst others. Moreover, much of the most elaborate and beautiful painting was carried out, like some of the finest ceramic decoration of other ages and countries, in a palette advantageously limited to a few red, black and white earthy pigments. Nevertheless, the Greek painting shows a restraint and precision which are in strong contrast with the bold freedom of much other ceramic decoration, such as that on the early Chinese pottery so greatly admired today. The forms, too, speak of lathe-turning, with its precision and refinement, rather than the potter's fingers manipulating the plastic clay. A disciplined austerity is indeed characteristic of all the finest Greek pottery, early and late.

Yet this quality is by no means peculiar to the Greek wares, and it cannot be pretended that we are dealing with a manifestation unique in kind, different from all other pottery, and therefore a field for the exercise of a privileged form of scholarship, from which, as from other Classical studies, profane persons must be excluded by a kind of academic class distinction. There is, on the contrary, every reason why Greek pottery in the wider sense should be brought within the scope of general ceramic history and connoisseurship, and therefore of this series. But it must be re-judged on its merits as ceramic art, without reference to its interest as the illustration of Greek life, thought and literature.

ix

FOREWORD

To make such a revaluation Mr. Arthur Lane is especially well qualified. A scholar at the British School at Athens before joining the staff of the Victoria and Albert Museum, he is in a position to reconcile the point of view of the Classical archaeologist with that of the connoisseur. He has here written an account of Greek pottery in which the wares of the Classical period are seen to fall into place as a culminating point in the development of an art practised in the various regions of the eastern Mediterranean over a period of more than six hundred years.

In no other book is the *art* of the Greek potter so comprehensively treated, with many masterpieces of shape, plastic decoration and painting impartially displayed. Complete specimens have in most cases been chosen for illustration, but to do justice to the painted vases it has been necessary to include (as indeed is customary) some photographs of details. But no use has been made of the usual drawn copies, since these produce a disastrous falsification in which the unique calligraphic quality of the originals is inevitably lost.

Thus the whole book, with its illustrations chosen for aesthetic merit alone, and its introductory essay with its broad and inspiring survey, should make a special appeal to the connoisseur and amateur and to the practical student of pottery, to whom many of the wares depicted may well come as exciting new discoveries.

W. B. H.

ACKNOWLEDGEMENTS

Photographs for this book have been obtained from nine different countries since the War, and I am deeply grateful to the individuals and to the authorities of numerous Museums who have thus helped me in these difficult times. Thanks are due above all to my friends in the Department of Greek and Roman Antiquities at the British Museum, who have made available many new and excellent photographs by Mr. C. O. Waterhouse. It will be seen that I have also enjoyed liberal support from the Metropolitan Museum, New York, and from the Museum of Fine Arts, Boston. More photographs have been lent or given by Professor J. D. Beazley, Dr. Hansjörg Bloesch, Mr. Robert Cook, Dr. Vagn Poulsen, Mr. Martin Robertson, and Mr. Charles Seltman.

As full annotation was ruled out in an essay of this kind, I hope that some readers will recognise my debt to the writers whose works I have pilfered. Dr. Hansjörg Bloesch of Berne and Mr. Robert Cook of Cambridge have been excellent guides to the more recent literature, and I have learnt more from conversation with them than I could hope to find in books. Mr. Cook has in addition been kind enough to read the text in proof and save me from many errors; for those that remain he is in no way responsible.

A. L.
August, 1947.

CONTENTS

CONTENTS

ILLUSTRATIONS

COLOUR PLATES

MONOCHROME PLATES
after page 64

1

HOW GREEK POTS WERE MADE AND PAINTED

In the art-room at the London Library, with all the books on Sculpture between them, there stand two separate sets of shelves. The one is labelled, Pottery and Porcelain; the other, Vases. What is a vase? The titles of the books and a sample of their contents suggest that, apart from a small initial contribution by the Proto-Elamites of Susa, all vases are pottery made by the Ancient Greeks. If we now move along to the section labelled Pottery and Porcelain, we see *Ancient Pottery*, by Walters. This, too, seems to be all about pottery made by the Greeks. But if we could consult the most comprehensive work on Greek pottery, that by Professor Ernst Pfuhl, we shall have to seek it under the category of books labelled 'Art'. Now why should Greek pots be 'vases', a phenomenon different in kind from all other pottery? Why should they form the staple of a huge book on Greek painting, in which their ceramic nature is virtually ignored? The answer is two-fold. Practically all writers on the subject have been archaeologists, unconcerned to discuss Greek art in relation to that of other civilizations, self-deprived of comparative standards in such matters as technique. Mr. Walters used to describe all ancient glazed vessels as 'porcelain'. On the other hand, writers on later ceramics have been daunted by the mass of esoteric literature surrounding Greek pottery, and have given only superficial attention to the pottery itself. They fail to find in it the aesthetic values they know; and have neither the patience nor the historic perception to recognize that other values, no less absolute, may have existed in the past. Such persons are apt to say that the decoration on Greek pottery is good as painting, but out of place on a pot; therefore the pots must be bad. But international learning ignores these unschooled twitterings, and continues to augment the great *Corpus Vasorum Antiquorum*, dedicated, in a prefatory note, to *l'archéologue occupé de céramographie*.

It is therefore difficult to enlist for Greek pottery the esteem of the ceramophile who is not occupied with archaeology, and whose mind is not predisposed by a tincture of classical learning. To the collector of

1

eighteenth-century porcelain those endless rows of red and black amphorai, closely packed on the Museum shelf according to size, will appear the essence of ceramic gloom. He cannot visualize a group of such pots drenched with water, standing on a stone pavement in the Mediterranean sun. But that is the way the Athenians commonly saw them, and those who have had this now unusual experience will not easily forget it. Again, these blatant shiny pots, looking as if made yesterday; what magic have they to compare with the mysterious Han granary jar, whose rather less hoary antiquity is attested by its decaying glaze and still adhering patches of genuine Chinese dirt? Where on what Attic urn is the romantic thumb-print of 'ceramic quality', for which some (not all) potters of Staffordshire and Japan are so applauded? No, the clichés of modern ceramic criticism do not fit Greek pottery, which is something quite outside the visual contexts to which we are accustomed.

A person able to appreciate the most varied manifestations of the potter's art may yet feel baffled in the presence of a good Attic 'vase'. This is no doubt partly due to an unconscious preconception. The fine pottery of modern civilization, and of China and the Near East since the early Middle Ages, is normally covered with a vitreous glaze. We associate unglazed pottery with primitive peoples, and are disconcerted to find it handled in a way that shows highly-sophisticated control of form and figurative decoration. It is here that a historical sense is needed. Glaze as we understand it was hardly known in Europe before the thirteenth century A.D., and painting on glazed pottery was not mastered till two centuries later. Greek potters cannot be blamed for their ignorance of modern techniques; they must be judged by their ability to use to full aesthetic and practical advantage the means they had available. It happens that a vitreous alkaline glaze was actually used on ornamental hand-made pottery in a country accessible to the Greeks—namely, Egypt; the potters of Asiatic Greece may even have experimented with this glaze and discarded it as unsuitable for the ends they had in view. The Greeks developed instead a technical medium for painting on useful wheel-made wares which passed out of human knowledge with the decline of Greco-Roman civilization. The nature of this medium has been re-discovered only within the last six years. Unless we understand it, we shall miss the point of the Greek contribution to the potter's art.

Let us therefore consider a few samples of what experts would call 'ripe' Greek pottery, and observe the results of this ancient painting-technique before analysing its method. The Attic vases shown on Plates 42, 43, 44 will serve. Preparation of clay, potter's wheel and kiln need no discussion—they followed the simple universal rules.

The pot-shape was built up from several horizontal sections; neck, foot, upper and lower body being thrown separately on the wheel and joined when sufficiently dry with a solution of clay 'slip'. The whole outer surface was then carefully pared down as the vase revolved on the wheel, but the horizontal ridges left by the thrower's fingers can still be felt inside. Measurement has shown that practically no two similar pots are exactly the same in size and shape, so the exquisite details of profile must have been individually trimmed with quite simple tools, and not with a template cut to give a mechanically uniform shape to a whole series of vessels. The finished pot is light in weight and soft enough to be easily scratched with a sharp knife, showing that the heat in the kiln was low—actually about 960° Centigrade. Nearly all Greek pots have sagged slightly out of shape in firing. Where visible, the fired Attic clay is of an uniform light orange-red colour, with a slight sheen. The black areas have a high polish akin to that produced with boot-blacking and quite different from the liquid appearance of modern glazes; the colouring matter is remarkably thin and well attached to the surface of the clay. Where possible, the blackening material was applied by brush to the pot spinning on the wheel, and the horizontal brush-marks remain visible. The black obviously did not become fluid and sticky while being fired, so no 'spurs' were necessary to keep the pots from adhering to the floor of the kiln. Lines drawn in black on the bare clay stand up perceptibly from the surface, and a slight groove down their middle suggests the use of a stiff bristle brush or feather dipped in a thick pigment. Less important details are drawn or washed in with a yellow-brown colour, apparently a dilution of the black. Some areas are painted white, obviously with some kind of pipeclay; this tends to flake off, leaving a dull patch on the black ground over which it is almost invariably laid. A colour ranging through pale violet to deep claret also has a clay base, tinted perhaps with red ochre or manganese; this develops a matt surface, and is again apt to wear away from its black ground.

Miss G. M. A. Richter, of the Metropolitan Museum, New York, has lucidly shown that the bright orange-red ground colour of Attic Greek pottery is due to the normal action of fire (1). Red potter's clay with a high content of ferric oxide of iron (Fe_2O_3) burns to a red colour if the kiln is well ventilated—if, in chemical terms, the carbon

---

(1) *The Craft of Athenian Pottery* (Metropolitan Museum of Art Publication), New York, 1923. An admirable short study that might be read with profit by those interested in pottery of any other kind. But Dr. Theodor Schumann's discoveries form a very necessary supplement.

released from the fuel by combustion can combine with two molecules of oxygen from the air to form carbon dioxide (CO_2). This process is called oxidation. If, on the other hand, the flow of air into the kiln is curtailed, the released carbon can only draw from the air one molecule of oxygen, with which it combines to form carbon monoxide (CO). This process is called reduction. But carbon monoxide, being very hungry for oxygen, will extract oxygen from wherever it can. And if the clay of the pots in the kiln contains ferric oxide, the carbon monoxide will take from it one molecule of oxygen and convert it into ferrous oxide ($CO + Fe_2O_3 = CO_2 + 2FeO$). Ferrous oxide is black, and according to the quantity of its presence in the clay the pots will emerge from the kiln a black or greyish colour. Clay containing no ferric oxide is usually not affected in colour by a reducing fire.

The brilliant black used on Attic and less successfully on other Greek pottery has puzzled modern potters and archaeologists for generations. It has been shown by analysis and synthesis that it contains an alkali (potash or soda), a clay (which would naturally comprise some silica), and black ferrous oxide of iron. But three things have hitherto lacked explanation. How was the high gloss obtained? How was the colour kept so stable that not even the finest lines of drawing lost definition by melting in the fire? And how was the intense black, which suggests a fire of extreme reducing action, produced conjointly with a bright redness of clay which could be due only to a strongly oxidising fire? These were truly lost secrets of Antiquity; but now at last we are in a fair way to understanding them, thanks to research carried out by Dr. Theodor Schumann at Heisterholz, near Minden, during the recent war.

Dr. Schumann's explanation has a classic simplicity based on his knowledge that the means disposed of by the ancient potters must themselves have been simple. At one time the black was often described as a 'varnish': this is impossible, for the oil base of any varnish would have perished in the fire. More recently the black has been called a 'glaze'; but this, too, is incorrect, for a glaze can only be formed when certain susceptible ingredients actually melt or fuse into a vitreous state owing to the action of the fire. As anyone can see, Greek black did not melt; Dr. Schumann pelted samples of Greek pottery in his experimental kiln while at the normal heat of firing with particles of sand, and observed that the particles did not stick to the painted surface.

A clue to the technique actually practised was found in the faint sheen apparent on the unpainted surfaces of Attic pottery. Miss Richter had attributed this to a polishing of the pot before it was painted; but in that case marks of the polishing tool should have been

4

visible, which they are not. The exceedingly smooth surface was in fact produced by methods of colloidal chemistry. However finely potter's clay is sifted by suspension in water, the clay particles each remain a coagulation of yet smaller particles. The coagulation can, however, be broken down by a process known as 'peptization', by the disintegrating action on the clay of certain chemicals, such as potash obtained from wood-ashes. A comparable process is that performed by the digestive juices on the food we eat. It is easy to see how the attention of early potters could have been drawn to the peculiar properties of potash; where kilns were fired by wood, ashes might at any time fall on the pots, and even the smoke from wood fuel might have a slightly 'peptic' effect. The recipe for procuring a really smooth surface at will would then consist in covering the vase before firing with a thin wash of the most finely-levigated clay, to which a proportion of potash had been added.

But 'peptization', if it breaks down existing aggregates of clay particles, does not prevent the smaller particles thus released from drifting together by magnetic attraction to form other aggregates of different shape. The surface of the pot might thus become smooth yet deformed, like the pebbled surface of a hen's egg. Fortunately, there exist substances known as 'protective colloids', which through their tanning action stabilize the particles after their release by the 'peptizing' agent, and prevent them from drifting about. A substance of this nature called 'humin' is found in organic matter, such as human or animal urine, gall, or sour wine. We know from the eleventh-century technical treatise of Theophilus, and from other early writers, that the black enamel pigment used for painting on medieval stained glass was mixed with urine or vinegar, which acted as a 'protective colloid'. It protected black lines painted on the glass from being dissolved away by the moisture of thinner washes of black colour laid over them; and at a later stage, while the painted glass panes were being fired in the kiln, it protected the fine detail from fusing and becoming blurred. Though written testimony is lacking, we must assume from the material evidence that the Greeks added a 'protective colloid', which by medieval analogy may have been urine or sour wine, to the thin clay-and-potash slip with which they covered their pots before painting.

The black painting itself was done in a thick, fluid pigment which, notably in the fine black lines on Attic red-figure wares, stands up in perceptible relief from the clay. It is glossy, and shows brush-marks clearly. So we can assume that the pigment contained clay particles to give it 'body'; potash to break up the particles and give a fine glossy surface; and a protective colloid (perhaps urine or vinegar) to act as a

5

fixative. The fluid may have been thickened and concentrated by evaporation. Now it has hitherto been believed that the ferrous oxide which gives the black colour was already an added ingredient in the pigment at the time of painting, for ferrous oxide can be found in a natural state. But Dr. Schumann has convincingly shown that the pigment actually contained no ingredients other than those we have described (with the proviso that the clay was always one containing iron); it was the same mixture as that used as a wash over the clay ground of the vase before painting, only more concentrated; and at the time of painting its colour was the same as that of the preliminary wash, but deeper in tone owing to the greater concentration of the coloured 'protective colloid'. This colour disappeared in the kiln because the organic matter to which it was due was consumed by the fire. As we shall now see, the black colour of the painting on the finished pot was produced by the fire acting in a different way on the painted and unpainted surfaces.

After painting, the pots were placed in the kiln and exposed to a clear, oxidizing fire which rose to a maximum of about 900–1000° Centigrade. If the clay contained much iron, as in Attica, it developed at this stage a bright red colour (see page 3); and the painting, too, became red, though darker in tone and glossier owing to the more concentrated state of its ingredients. The red 'terra sigillata' of Roman times developed its colour through the action of a purely oxidizing fire on a surface wash of the same nature as was used by the Greeks to paint their pots. But Greek pottery had to undergo further stages of firing. When the oxidizing stage was judged complete, the opposite process of reduction was begun. Greek kilns so far discovered usually have two separate channels leading to the firing-chamber. It is probable that one was used for the oxidizing fire and stoked with dry wood. This entrance was doubtless closed during the reducing process, when the second channel was used to introduce either a bowl of water or a damp fuel such as green wood, which when starved of air would give off an excess of carbon monoxide in the form of smoke. The reducing fire converted the red ferric oxide to black ferrous oxide (see p. 4); in other words, the painted and unpainted areas of the pots developed a black colour in differing tones. Now began yet a third stage of firing—that of re-oxidation. The damp fuel or bowl of water was raked out and a clear, well-ventilated fire re-introduced. Once more the pots began to redden, as oxygen penetrated the clay and formed red ferric oxide. But the wash applied to the surface of the pots acted as a protective layer that resisted penetration by oxygen in varying degrees. Where the wash was very thin, namely, on the unpainted areas of the surface, the resistance was slight, and these areas reddened rapidly. Where the layer of wash was thick, as in the painted areas and lines, the oxygen had greater difficulty in penetrating to the more densely compacted particles of clay and combining with their black ferrous oxide content to form red ferric oxide. The fire had to be raked out of the kiln at the point when the unpainted parts had already become red and the blackened, painted, parts had not yet had time to change colour. We can recognize the results of correct timing by the potter; and we can also recognize his errors. On some pots the parts intended to be black have become partially or wholly red, through being left too long in the re-oxidizing fire. Or there may be red spots or patches in the black, probably because at these points the 'painting' was not applied thickly enough to set up an effective resistance to penetration by oxygen. In Attic red-figure wares the isolated black lines drawn across the clay, and the edges of the black background around the figures, both needed special reinforcement; for at these points the oxygen could penetrate the clay and attack the painting from the back. On black-figure wares, especially the carelessly-painted ones where no such precautions were taken, we often see the sharpness of the silhouette fading away at the edges into yellow-brown. It should be clearly recognized that the hard, deliberate character of most Greek vase-painting is partly due to the necessity of having the 'paint' thick at the edges of the design. If the pigment had been thin and the brush-strokes rapid, the edges would have been nibbled away by the re-oxidizing fire.

In some kinds of Greek pottery, for example those made of or coated with a whitish clay containing little or no iron, perhaps two phases only were needed in the firing; an oxidizing phase to 'cook' the pot, and a reducing phase to bring down the reddened painting from the condition of red ferric oxide to that of black ferrous oxide. The Corinthian pieces with black painting on a greenish-white ground may have been fired thus. But other Corinthian pieces show orange-red painting on a warm buff ground; and this state may have been reached either in a single oxidizing phase, or else in a third, re-oxidizing phase carried to excess.

Note: Since this chapter was written, Miss Richter has shown me sample tablets of pottery made and painted by Dr. Schumann in accordance with the methods he had inferred from his experiments. The Westphalian clay he used burns slightly paler than Attic clay, but otherwise the finished results so closely resemble genuine Attic pottery as to leave no doubt that the samples correctly illustrate the ancient technique in every stage.

2
USE, SHAPES, AND ORNAMENT

It has been necessary to dwell thus long on technical processes, because these qualified the nature of Greek pottery, not only in its utilitarian aspect, but also in its aesthetic range. Most Greek pots that survive entire were found buried with the dead—in tombs in Italy, Sicily, Asia Minor, and the East Mediterranean islands, as well as in mainland Greece itself. The richest finds of Attic pottery were made during the '20s and '30s of the nineteenth century round Vulci, some sixty miles north-west of Rome, where Lucien Bonaparte and his family throve by tomb-robbing and selling the produce on the international antique-market. Archaeologists have found quantities of less well-preserved pottery on the sites of Greek temples and shrines, where they had been dedicated as offerings to the god. But the vessels deliberately made for funerary or votive purposes were few in number, and can at once be recognized by the special character of their shape and decoration. The ancient Etruscans and others imported Greek pottery for its excellent quality as useful ware. Of the numerous vessels illustrated in this book, we can say with confidence that all but three were intended for normal domestic use.(1) Similar vessels were constantly depicted by the pot-painters either in the hands of the user, or hanging ready on a nail in the wall. Within the period here surveyed, the 'vase' as a household ornament was a conception unknown to the Greeks. It is, indeed, by an odd inversion of propriety that the word 'vase', with its modern connotation of ornamental un-usefulness, has attached itself to Greek pottery, and that as a result of antiquarian habit we can hardly think of this pottery outside a Museum (2). Be-

(1) Plates 5B, 51, 90 show funeral vases. Many of the pots found in tombs show obvious signs of wear; some have even been riveted in ancient times. Dr. Bloesch informs me that he has seen vessels from graves that had deliberately been made useless by having a hole bored through them, after their useful life above ground was over.

(2) 'Vasa' in good Latin can mean both pots and plates made of any material, regarded as utensils—what we would call 'pots and pans'. From 'vascellum', the colloquial diminutive of 'vas', we derive our

cause they aimed at and obtained good surface finish and reasonable-
ness of shape, the Greek potters have even been accused of striving
after a 'Museum effect'—as if smoothness, and therefore cleanliness,
had not been a constant objective of potters from prehistoric times
until our own industrial age, whenever they have made clay vessels
to eat and drink from. Too few people today are conscious of the very
close affinity that exists between the best modern table-wares and
those of Ancient Greece; both show the same intelligent regard for
function, and both express a will to form, not through mass and
volume, but through the vitality of a linear profile. Nor is this
accidental; we have not yet discovered a better range of forms for
domestic use than those of Josiah Wedgwood, the first great industrial
potter; and his ideas were profoundly influenced by his study of Greek
pottery. It is odd to think that the 'blue jasper' wares he valued so
highly quite lack the Greek spirit that informed his 'useful' cream-
coloured earthenware.

For good or bad, then, utility was a discipline that the Greek potter
had to observe. He was not free to pursue the ultimate refinements or
extravagances of pure ceramic form for their own sake. That could
only happen in such a civilization as the Chinese, where practical
requirements were ignored in the art-pottery made for religious
ceremony, for burial with the dead, or for the aesthetic enjoyment of
Imperial collectors. Many of the Greek pot-shapes remained essentially
the same for centuries, because they were so well suited to the needs
of Greek society; and the potter thus had to express his changing
sense of form through variations within a fairly narrow range. By far
the majority of the basic shapes were intended for holding wine,
water, oil, perfume and other liquids. Cups were by our standards
often surprisingly large; but we all know that in ancient times a
ceremonial cup would be passed round the whole company of guests.
It was the Greek custom to drink the wine mixed with at least two
parts of water. Mixing and pouring called for a diversity of appropriate vessels; the covered *amphora* for temporary storage of wine, in
common with cereals and other food; the *krater* or large mixing bowl;
the *kyathos* or ladle for dipping the mixture off into jugs (*oinochoai*) or
directly into the cups. The latter, whether deep with flat bases
(*kotylai*) or wide and shallow with pedestal bases (*kylikes*), almost
invariably had horizontal handles, for when lying on a couch it was
easier to lift a large, heavy cup with the thumb than with the fore-
finger. The function of the three-handled water-pitcher (*hydria*) is

---

word 'vessel'—not quite such a useful word as 'vase' would have been
had its original meaning been kept.

9

self-evident from the illustration on Plate 46. Olive oil, rubbed on and scraped off with a metal blade, took the place of soap; it was carried in small bottles (*aryballoi*, *lekythoi*, *alabastra*) suspended by a string from the wrist. They, like the small toilet-boxes (*pyxides*), often show astonishing precision of shape and delicacy of ornament; one could hardly believe that earthenware lacking a true glaze could be so agreeable to handle. By modern standards, the Greek black 'glaze' had certain shortcomings, even when used by the exceptionally competent potters of Attica. Though indestructible by acid, heat, or damp, it was never completely impervious to liquids. The Greeks, with their simple household arrangements, can hardly have minded this; indeed, they showed their indifference by leaving large areas of their pots unglazed, and therefore more susceptible to a gradual seepage. The cooling effect of surface-evaporation may even have been thought advantageous in such a warm climate.

The Greek potter was fully aware of more serious weaknesses in his materials. With only simple kilns and non-refractory clays at his disposal, he could not fire his earthenware to a high degree of hardness. The best Attic and Corinthian ware is surprisingly tough, but it lacks tensile strength. And so we find that vulnerable points of a vessel, such as the lip or edge of the foot, were reinforced in thickness to make them stronger; and it is a measure of Greek taste and ingenuity that this very thickening, which might so easily have appeared clumsy, was converted by curves and mouldings into a refinement of profile that could be justified on aesthetic grounds alone. One may contrast the lack of ceramic realism shown by the makers of faïence and delft-ware in the seventeenth and eighteenth centuries; they, too, worked in soft earthenware, but in emulation of Chinese porcelain made their edges so thin that the vessels chipped or split at the slightest accidental blow.

Chinese potters of all dates have disliked putting handles on their pots, because paired handles unpleasantly punctuate in a two-dimensional plane the three-dimensional ovoid or globular volume that is for them the ideal ceramic form. The Greeks, like later Europeans, were not prepared to sacrifice practical convenience to aesthetic purism and decided for handles—big handles, apt to the hand, and so strong that they could not be knocked off without taking a large part of the vessel with them. It is a delight to observe how by bold tapering and contrapuntal curve the handle was often made to appear an inseparable organic part of the whole form (1). The idea may be carried yet further by the way the handles are painted; on

(1) See especially Plates 39B, 68A, 74, 75.

their outer surface the decoration assimilates itself to that of the body, while the inner surface and the part of the vessel that they span is deliberately left unpainted. One recognizes intuitively how the sense of attachment is thereby symbolized; such unpainted areas are, in physiological metaphor, the mucous membrane of the vase.

A loose generalization is sometimes made, to the effect that Greek potters habitually derived their shapes from metal vases. In a broad sense this idea is absurd; if at a certain time well-established work-shops for pottery and metalwork exist, and a given form could be equally well expressed in either medium, we are quite unjustified in assuming without specific evidence that the form first took concrete shape in this or that material. Form can be arrived at by empirical methods, as a happy accident supervening on the experimental manipulation of a material; or it may be a concept in the mind, that struggles into tangible shape through whatever channels it can. Their literature, philosophy and art show that the conceptual attitude to form was more deeply engrained in the Greeks than in any other people of whom we know. To judge from the 'geometrical' decoration of their early pottery, they might at that time have been totally blind to the surrounding world of natural phenomena. It was impossible for them to perceive an object, and then fluently translate this percept into a representational work of art. After perception came the agonizing mental process of creating the concept; what the early con-cept of 'man' looked like we can see on a 'geometric' vase (1). Early Greek sculpture came out of the artist's mind; only by comparing his work with the living human body was the sculptor able gradually to correct and re-shape his concept into the powerful instrument of anatomical knowledge that lends such authority to the idealistic sculpture of the fifth century. Plant-forms had little interest for the early Greek artist, who here took over his concepts ready-made from the older arts of Asia and Egypt and modified them only for decorative convenience. The introspective, conceptual habit of the Greek will to form, already apparent in the ornament of the 'geometric' vases, achieved its most awe-inspiring manifestation in the major art of architecture—in the Doric temple. Here the concept must have been based on perception of the earliest Greek temples, with their tree-trunk columns, horizontal architraves, and gabled thatch-roofs. But when it issues forth in stone the intellectual translation is seen to have been formidably complete; it has borrowed nothing further from nature; yet for the mechanical tensions of structural engineering, which could be solved in purely geometrical terms, it has substituted

(1) *Plate* 5B.

a system of imaginative tensions, which are solved in terms of geo-metry modified in an organic sense. The circular, fluted column, with its profile tapering upwards in a hyperbolic curve; the inward tilting of the corner columns; the slight upward bulge of the stylobate to-wards the centre, are 'refinements' unnecessary to engineering; and it is they that give to a building such as the Parthenon its extra-ordinary feeling of life.

The forms of Greek vases are drawn from this world of vitalized geometry. Sometimes there are more overt organic allusions—for example, the monstrous eyes and ears painted on the kylix (1). In aesthetic effect this cup is curiously like a modern high-speed air-craft; both have the same bracing sense of tension against outer space, in one case real, in the other, imagined. We may further compare the streamlined profile of Attic red-figured vases (2). Nothing could differ more from the static forms of Chinese pottery, whose curves expand and contract in relation to the inner space they enclose—never in opposition to an imagined pressure from outside. The Chinese and the Greek potter stand at the two poles of ceramic temperament, yet both operate within the limits prescribed for their craft; and of the two it is the Greek who remains truer to the stern logic of the potter's wheel. We find no square or oval pots in Greece, nor is the circle broken into petal-shaped lobes. The mouldings and members of a Greek pot-form were fashioned with various cutting tools as the half-dry pot spun on the wheel; even the iron-black colour retains the horizontal striations caused by a steady brush applied to the revolving surface. This hori-zontal cutting action, which results in a smooth surface suitable for painted decoration, is almost universally evident in Greek pottery until about the end of the fifth century B.C. One cannot imagine the developed red-figure forms carried out in any medium other than clay trimmed on the wheel (3). Where smooth vessels of similar form are found in clay and metal, we can hardly help concluding that the Greek will to form had often given priority to clay as its favourite means of expression. Decoration in low relief is peculiarly suited to metalwork, and when, in the fourth century, we find such decoration encroaching on the surface of clay vessels (4), we may rightly assume that the metal-workers have taken over the lead formerly held by the potters. In fact, the potentialities of painted decoration on pottery had by then been exhausted. From about 400 B.C. till the end of the Roman Empire the aesthetic of metalwork, expressed in relief-decoration, retained its ascendancy over the more sophisticated kinds of pottery,

(1) *Plate* 55B; (2) *Plates* 68, 74–81; (3) *Plates* 68A, 74–84; (4) *Plate* 96.

such as the so-called 'Megarian bowls' (1) of Hellenistic times and the red-glazed 'terra sigillata' of the Roman Empire.

But even in his heyday the Greek potter was inclined to hanker after certain elegant trimmings more proper to the metal medium than his own. In metalwork, handles were made separately from the vessels, to which they were subsequently attached with rivets. It was difficult to conceal the join; the smooth transition possible in clay was out of the question. The metal handle was therefore treated as a separate member, and its articulations emphasized by boldly-modelled ornament—a spreading palmette, a human head, or a knuckle-bone expanding to wide disks at the ends. We often find this handle-treatment imitated in archaic Greek pottery of the late seventh and early sixth century; and an Athenian potter named Nikosthenes, who worked in the second half of the sixth century, betrayed his medium and exhibited his personal bad taste by habitually making whole pots look as if designed for metal (2). But these borrowings from metal-work generally went no further than marginal eccentricity on other-wise sound ceramic shapes; they disappeared as the Attic potters developed their idea of tapering handles organically proceeding from the pot. Oddly enough the painters remained more conservative than the potters; the palmette or circle of tongue pattern sometimes lingered on as a painted vestige at the base of the handle with quite literal reference to its metal origin; but often it underwent happier, more imaginative development as freely-painted ornament (3).

Most of the Greek pots in our museums are finely painted (the badly painted or undecorated pieces have been quietly suppressed by the selective taste of excavators and museum officials). Nearly all the voluminous literature is about the painting that happens to be on the pots, rather than about the pots themselves. For this there is some excuse—the painting can be so extraordinarily good, and so little of ancient painting survives in any other form. Moreover, until the fifth century, artists had neither the technique nor the breadth of vision necessary for painting on a large scale, so into the miniature-painting on vases they put their very best. In this they resembled the manu-script-painters of the Middle Ages: with the manuscripts preserved, we scarcely miss the less accomplished mural paintings that have perished. But between 480 and 450 B.C. wall-painting at last assumed its true position as a major art through the work of Polygnotus, the

---

(1) *Plate* 95B; (2) *Plate* 53. The amphora on Plate 64, made by Pamphaios, is a softened version of Nikosthenes' favourite shape, lacking the horizontal ribs in relief round the shoulder; (3) *Plates* 58, 62B, 81, 87 (vestiges); 39B, 40D, 42, 43, 55B (painted development).

first 'Old Master' among the Greeks. Vase-painting inevitably became an activity for the second-rate; it bore to Polygnotus and his successors roughly the same relation as the *'istoriato'* painting on sixteenth-century Italian maiolica bears to the frescoes of Raphael. The bad art of Antiquity is no less tedious than the bad art of more recent times, and in this study we shall hardly glance beyond the point where the Greek potters had reached the summit of their powers. Their technique, of marvellous perfection when properly used, revealed its narrowness in clumsy or careless hands. It was the tragedy of post-classical Greek art that too high a standard had been set; an adult and sophisticated attitude was all-pervading; and very rarely does one find the ingenuous charm of a humble popular art (1).

The subject-matter and styles of pot-painting will be further discussed in the next chapter, but a few generalizations may be permitted here. Texture, colour, and decoration are all elements that may contribute to excellence in pottery; form alone is essential. And in their preoccupation with perfect form Greek potters were quite uninfluenced by the thought that the pots might have to carry painted decoration. Anyone who has been present at the excavation of a Greek site will confirm that finely-painted vessels were far outnumbered by those with slighter ornament or with a coat of plain iron-black. It was therefore left to the painter to adapt his decoration to the shape as best he could.

For close on six centuries he was guided by certain basic principles. First, that painting should emphasize the continuity of the pot surface (including the handles); should reinforce, as it were, the defence against outer space. In many 'geometric' pots this idea was carried so far that the painting looks like a skin-tight garment, a patterned football-jersey and a pair of dark shorts (2). When animal and human figures superseded geometrical ornament, the gaps between them had to be bridged by rosettes and other quite meaningless 'filling-ornaments' (3). The later Attic black-figure painters skilfully disguised their filling as leafy tree-stems, or as inscriptions— many of these were nonsensical, and owed their presence to decorative needs alone (4). In its most sophisticated development Attic red-figure painting put up a defence as complete as the earliest geometric, for the whole surface, apart from the figures and borders, was sealed by a solid wall of black (5).

Arrangement of ornament on the surface followed the same

(1) As, for example, in the toy cup, *Plate* 95A; (2) e.g. *Plate* 10A; (3) *Plates* 17, 18, 25, 27A; (4) *Plates* 21A, 39B, 43, 52A; (5) *Plates* 78, 79, 82, 84.

principles as Greek architecture—a number of superimposed courses with strong horizontal emphasis, admitting a fairly emphatic vertical punctuation in the main course. The main frieze of human figures painted on a pot had the same part to play in the total composition as the colonnade in a Greek temple. Owing to the presence of handles, the main painted frieze was usually subject to interruptions, and it is interesting to see how tactfully Attic painters stressed or mitigated these in sympathy with the shape of the vase. The neck of one standard amphora-shape is strongly articulated at its junction with the shoulder; so the horizontal line of its base is echoed by bands of ornament lower down the body, and the painted ornament depending from the handle is purposely lightened to avoid the intrusion of any strong vertical accent (1). The other standard Attic amphora-shape has a long unbroken curve from lip to base (2). Bands of ornament are therefore largely suppressed, since their horizontal movement would war with the vertical movement of the profile; and the painted figures are confined in a panel whose side lines at once echo the curve of the vase, and permit a vertical rectangle of black to continue the up-and-down movement of the handles when the vase is seen from the side.

When he started making a statue, the early Greek sculptor first marked on the face of his stone block the outline of the figure as seen from the front. He then moved round and marked on the side of the block the figure as seen in profile. Formal progress in scuplture depended eventually on the sculptor's ability to bridge and at length abolish the transition between two planes set at right angles. The early painter, on the other hand, could select distinctive items from the two viewpoints and combine them in one figure; head and legs in profile, the triangular torso in full view. The third dimension gave him no trouble, for the figure was regarded as flat. A team of horses or a rank of warriors abreast were arranged like a spread hand of playing cards (3). Even a four-horse chariot seen from the front could be telescoped into the scheme by showing only the extreme edges of the superposed planes; and frontal faces appeared quite early (4), though for some reason Greek artists found them difficult and therefore reserved them for grotesques—silens or gorgons. This convention of the flat figure was admirably suited to pot-decoration, for it carried no sense of spatial penetration into the surface of the vessel. It sur-

---

(1) *Plates* 42, 43, 48. The less sensitive 'Chalkidian' potters tended to overlook this point of 'syntax', carrying the main frieze right round the vase and thus destroying its vertical cohesion—*Plate* 56; (2) *Plates* 44, 65; (3) *Plates* 23c, 24b, 35b, 37b, 45b; (4) *Colour Plate* B (page 42); *Plates* 36a, 28b.

15

vived for artistic reasons long after knowledge of anatomy and perspective had made it out-of-date. From the last quarter of the sixth century Attic red-figure pot-painters explored every detail of human anatomy and attitude; they showed one leg in profile, another full on, and folded the arms and torso backwards and forwards without regard to the position of head and legs. But so long as foreshortening confined itself to a combination of flat frontal and profile views, overlapping where necessary, the situation was safe. What killed Greek vase-painting was the admission of the three-quarters view. It made further pretence about spatial recession impossible; the pot-surface was visibly broken through. Four-horse chariots in three-quarter view appeared sporadically on Attic black-figure pots before the end of the sixth century; but the red-figure painters agreed to avoid this solecism for another fifty years before they too succumbed and made the three-quarter view an universal cliché (1). By then monumental painting had suggested an even more formidable explosive; perhaps it was the great Polygnotus of Thasos who first painted figures standing in a landscape at different levels, to give them recession. Following his example, pot-painters, too, abandoned the uniform base-line for the figures, which now floated vaguely up and down the pot-surface (2); it was as if the columns of a temple had started jumping from their foundations. Pot-painting no longer subscribed to the formal unity of the pot and thereby forfeited its right to exist.

It had been no mean achievement of the Greek potters to reconcile the threefold demands of utility, of form, and of decoration, when each demanded so much. Potters now have an easier task. They need satisfy no more than two demands at once; utility and form in wares intended for use; form and decoration in art-pottery intended for looking at. And it is a convention of our day that not even ornamental pottery should be too heavily charged with ideas; we prefer to see in it the easy, sensuous qualities of colour, texture, and rhythmic design, innocent of ulterior meaning. How often is it said that Greek vase-painting is excellent, but too good to be on pottery. Yet it was designed for pottery, and for technical reasons could have existed nowhere else. If we are honest with ourselves, we must admit that early Greek pottery makes such a formidable challenge to our minds and senses that we are rather afraid of it. We stand at the very end of a great phase of representational art that began with the Renaissance, if not before. The eye tires with the complexity of the visible world; of the human figure we have had more than enough. We may even be past the threshold of a new Byzantine epoch, where regulation

---

(1) *Plates* 86, 87, 94; (2) *Plates* 87, 94.

supplants the individual will in society, where disembodied symbols and geometric forms are all we can bear to look at in art. But the archaic Greek artist had only just discovered that 'there are many wonders, and none more wonderful than man'. His vases would have enchanted fifteenth-century Florence; us, in our decrepitude, they mock.

3
HISTORICAL OUTLINE

Sometimes in small bands who settled peaceably, sometimes in great waves that disrupted all previous settlement, the many tribes of Hellenes expanded southwards through what we now call Greece. Their migrations may have begun about 1700 B.C. The Minoan civilization of Crete was then at its height, secure in its sea-power, freely creative in all branches of art. When the kings of Mycenae on the Greek mainland came to dominate a loose confederacy of lesser chieftains, they derived the equipment of culture from Crete. At length, about 1400 B.C., they set sail for Crete and overthrew the Minoan Kingdom. A common Mycenaean (or so-called 'Helladic') culture now spread throughout the Eastern Mediterranean.

Hellenic peoples still pressed down into Greece from the north, or sought fresh land in the Aegean Islands and the foreshores of Asia Minor. The Trojan War, sung by Homer, was an episode of this expansion; perhaps about 1200–1150 B.C., Agamemnon of Mycenae led a federation of bronze-clad chieftains to crush a centre of Asiatic resistance. But Agamemnon's successors at Mycenae in turn succumbed to a final wave of northern invaders called the Dorians, formidable warriors with superior swords of iron. The Dorians slowly blotted out the old Minoan-Mycenean-Helladic civilization of the Aegean. When a new Iron-Age culture started, from very humble beginnings, it was definitely Greek.

About this time, say 1100–900 B.C., three branches of the Hellenic race won homes on the Asia Minor coast: to the north the Aeolians, to the south the Dorians; in the middle the more active Ionians, whose chief city was Miletus. These settlers intermarried with their Asiatic neighbours, and mixed blood may have aided the precocious intellectual development of 'Eastern Greece'. Here the Greek voice first spoke to the world through the mouths of Homer, the lyric poets of Lesbos, and the natural philosophers of Ionia. And the Ionians contributed much to Greek art. They seem to have inherited something of the Minoan delight in fleeting appearance, in surface pattern, in vivacious movement; and from the art of their Asiatic neighbours they derived a feeling for soft and rounded plastic forms. A contrasting

18

preference for hard, close-knit, intellectually-conceived forms developed in the Peloponnese and other lands where the people were mainly Dorian. It was eventually left to the Athenians, themselves Ionian by race, to reconcile and fuse the Dorian and Ionian strains in the mature art of the fifth century.

Greece again expanded in the two centuries 750–550 B.C. Colonies were sent out by individual city-states of Eastern and Mainland Greece, seeking land to cultivate as well as trade. In the Eastern Mediterranean the chain extended all round the coasts of Thrace and the Black Sea, and along southern Asia Minor as far as Poseideion (Al Mina) near Syrian Antioch (1). Two settlements lodged in Egypt, Cyrene and two other colonies in Libya. To the west, the chain embraced the heel and toe of Italy as far as Cyme, near Naples, and the whole coast of Sicily except the western corner. The East-Greek cities sent even more colonies to the west than Mainland cities such as Corinth; indeed, the most astonishing venture was that of Phocaea, which from Asia Minor colonized Monoikos (Monaco), Nicaea (Nice), Antipolis (Antibes), Massilia (Marseilles), and even Emporiae (Ampurias) in Spain. Greek merchantmen swept the Black Sea and Mediterranean from end to end, in rivalry with the Phoenicians based on Tyre and Sidon in the east, and on Carthage, Tunisia, and western Sicily in the west. Native peoples were on the whole friendly to the small Greek city-states on their coasts, for the advantages of trade were mutual. In return for minerals and agricultural produce, Greek ships brought wine, oil, and manufactured articles. Of the last, good pottery was one of the most considerable items. It has been found wherever there were Greek colonies and far in their hinterland.

Historically speaking, fine pottery made by the Greeks between 1000 and 400 B.C. falls into four main groups. Before 700 B.C. wares painted in brown or black monochrome with *geometric* decoration were made in many localities and exported only within a narrow radius. In the seventh century, pottery, and Greek art generally, underwent profound modifications owing to trade contacts with Egypt, Phoenicia, and the inland peoples of Asia. Textiles, carved ivory, and above all metal objects found their way into the cities of Eastern and Mainland Greece, where their stylized ornament of human, animal and plant-forms encouraged potters to abandon the old geometrical designs. This *orientalising* phase of the seventh century saw also the introduction of polychrome painting and the 'black figure' technique, wherein black-painted silhouette figures were enriched with detail

(1) There is some evidence of another early Greek settlement in Syria at Tell Sukas, seventeen miles south-east of Latakia.

incised in the yet unfired clay. Eastern Greece preferred pure brush-painting; on the Mainland, Corinth in particular developed the incised black-figure. The main factories now supplied a very wide export-trade. The sixth century, until about 530, was the *floruit* of the mature *black-figure* technique; Athenian potters now captured the foreign markets from Corinth; and the brush-painted wares of Eastern Greece fell into decline. From about 530 until 400 B.C. Athenian pottery alone deserves consideration, most of it being painted in the *red-figure* technique of figures reserved in a black-painted ground.

Dates assigned to the vessels here illustrated may seem too confidently precise. They are mostly based on archaeological convention, which is by no means unanimous. The archaeologist works by comparative methods; using the internal evidence of style and technique, he sorts the surviving vessels and fragments into groups that may or may not be attributable to a certain manufacturing centre, and then seeks to establish the chronological order of pieces within each group and their relative chronology *vis-à-vis* the other groups. This subjective procedure is to a large extent supplemented by the objective evidence of archaeological excavation. Earlier wares normally lie in the deeper stratified layers of a continuously occupied site; and the graves in an ancient cemetery offer successive groups of pottery, often of varying origin, that must have been buried simultaneously and probably were made not long beforehand. Potters' or painters' signatures hardly appear except on Attic pottery of the late black-figure and red-figure phases, but by then progress in representing the human form was so rapid, and the scope for idiosyncrasies of style so wide, that even a novice can recognize the artistic personality of certain painters. Attic red-figure painting has been a lifelong study for an archaeologist and connoisseur of genius, Professor J. D. Beazley of Oxford. Aided by other archaeologists, by inscriptions on the pottery, and above all by an unrivalled sense for style, Professor Beazley has been able to attribute upwards of fifteen thousand red-figure vases to individual painters, showing how each man developed, and with him the whole Attic school.

But even Professor Beazley seldom mentions dates (in writing). In fact, the whole system of relative dating in sequence, on stylistic and archaeological evidence combined, may be compared to a concertina. We seldom know when the instrument is fully expanded, or when half-closed; some phases of ceramic development may have extended over a very long period, others may have been compressed into a short span of years. What we need is a measuring-rod of absolute historical dates that may be applied to points in the relative sequence. And as the Greeks were late in adopting a rational system of chronology, the measuring-rod is defective. Absolute dates for the Trojan war rest on doubtful later traditions; we do not know in what years the Dorians arrived; the earliest 'protogeometric' pottery represents the upper end of our archaeological concertina, wobbling freely in spite of rival theories as to how it may be controlled. Apart from an occasional Egyptian scarab, found entombed among Greek pottery, our first landmark for absolute dating is the traditional sequence of dates given by much later ancient historians for the founding of certain Greek colonies in Sicily and Italy (e.g. Syracuse 734 B.C., Megara Hyblaea 730, Taranto 706). Greek pots found in graves at such colonies show a style-sequence that would agree with the date-sequence given by the historians; so these dates are accepted as approximately correct. Another useful absolute date is given by the Siphnian treasure-house at Delphi, built shortly before 525 B.C., and decorated with reliefs probably by the Athenian sculptor Endoios. The style of the sculpture closely resembles that of the earliest Attic red-figure vase-painting (1). A more precise date arises from the ravaging of the Athenian Acropolis by the Persian invaders in 480 B.C. When the Athenians later returned they threw the debris of the destroyed temple-offerings over the cliff-edge of the citadel or into the foundations of their new buildings. Modern archaeologists have dug up the debris, and can with confidence say that the red-figure and black-figure potsherds found in it must be dated before 480 B.C.

---

(1) *Plates* 62, 63.

4
NOTES ON THE ILLUSTRATIONS

Pre-Greek Pottery

Plate 1. Jug painted in dark brown on buff, from Egypt. Made in Crete: 'Late Minoan I'; about 1550–1450 B.C. Ht. $9\frac{7}{8}$ in. Marseilles Museum.
Plate 2. (*a*) Stem-cup (kylix) painted in brown-red on pale yellowish clay. From Kalymnos. 'Late Helladic III'; about 1375–1200 B.C. Ht. $7\frac{1}{2}$ in.
Plate 2. (*b*) Mixing-bowl (krater), painted in purple-brown on buff clay. From Enkomi (Cyprus). 'Late Helladic III'; about 1375–1200 B.C. Ht. $10\frac{1}{2}$ in. Both, British Museum.

Cretan pottery of the Middle Minoan period (about 1800 B.C.) was often painted in matt white and red on a matt black ground—the 'Kamares' style named after a cave in Crete where many examples were found. Matt-painted polychrome wares were also made in Syria and Mesopotamia. But in the Late Minoan and Late Helladic (or Mycenean) pottery of the Aegean polychrome effects were abandoned in favour of monochrome painting on the buff clay. The pigment, burning orange-red, brown, or black, already had the gloss found in later Greek pottery (see p. 4). The Late Minoan jug (1) was made on the 'slow' wheel, and is consequently so irregular in shape as to suggest hand-modelling. Its top-heavy, exaggerated proportions recall the Minoan architectural column, tapering downwards from a wide capital to a narrow base. In the two later pieces (2) greater regularity of contour suggests more adept use of the potter's wheel, though we still miss the precision of true Greek pottery. On the Cretan jug nautilus-shells, admirably summarized from direct observation of nature, swim all over the surface without regard to the shape of the vessel. The cuttle-fish on the cup is at once more stylized and more consciously adapted to its position in the decorative scheme; and the bull, however anarchic its personal anatomy, is at any rate kept firmly within its frieze. Human figures, warriors, and chariots were often painted in the same loose manner.

(1) *Plate* 1; (2) *Plate* 2.

Proto-geometric Greek Pottery

Plate 3. (*a*) Cup, painted in brown-black on light yellow-brown clay. From a grave in the Kerameikos cemetery at Athens. Attic: about 950–900 B.C. Ht. $5\frac{1}{8}$ in.

Plate 3. (*b*) Amphora, painted in brown-black on light yellow-brown clay. From a grave in the Kerameikos cemetery at Athens. Attic; about 1000–950 B.C. Ht. $15\frac{5}{8}$ in. Both, Athens.

Plate 4. Amphora, painted in black on yellow-brown clay. From a grave in the Kerameikos cemetery at Athens. Attic; about 950–900 B.C. Ht. $14\frac{1}{8}$ in. Athens.

The arrival of the Dorians, of the Iron Age, did not instantaneously efface the pre-Greek Helladic civilization. Tendencies that crystallized in the 'Protogeometric' Greek pottery of about 1000–900 B.C. were at work long before; but for the sake of contrast, in shape, ornament and composition, the gradual intermediate stages between our Plates 1–2 and 3–4 must here be omitted. These pots from an Athenian cemetery were all made on a swiftly-turning wheel. They have thus a crispness of contour not found in earlier wares, but almost universal in later Greek pottery. The centre of gravity is placed lower, giving greater stability, and the spreading necks or feet are sharply articulated at their junction with the body. Circles or half-circles, precisely compass-drawn, replace the sprawling human or animal figures, and there are already the beginnings of 'geometric' ornament proper. Some large pots still show a predominantly light ground (1) but on smaller ones the greater part of the surface is painted black. The black has a 'defensive' quality; it is to be imagined as a kind of sheath enclosing the clay, which is only exposed with caution in narrow bands or rectangular panels each laced over with simple painted designs. In some parts of the Greek world, for example, in Rhodes, this sombre style lasted for a very long time. Progress consisted in breaking down the solid black into an even half-tone of hatched linear designs that covered more and more of the vase, yet nowhere admitted a significant gap in texture.

---

(1) *Plate* 3B.

Geometric Pottery

Plate 5. (*a*) Cup, painted in brown-black on light yellow-brown clay. Attic; ninth century B.C. Ht. $6\frac{5}{8}$ in. Athens.

Plate 5. (*b*) Detail from a large amphora used as a grave-monument, painted with a funeral scene. Attic; eighth century B.C. Athens, National Museum.

Plate 6. Amphora, painted in brown-black on yellow-brown clay. Attic; eighth century B.C. Ht. $23\frac{5}{8}$ in. Boston, Museum of Fine Arts.

Plate 7. (*a*) Covered box (pyxis), painted in brown-black on light yellow-brown clay. From Athens. Attic; eighth century B.C. Ht. $9\frac{3}{4}$ in. Leyden, Museum of Archaeology.

Plate 7. (*b*) Cup (lekane), painted in brown-black on light yellow-brown clay. Attic; eighth century B.C. Diam. at lip $5\frac{6}{10}$ in. British Museum.

Plate 8. Jug (oinochoe), painted in brown-black on light yellow-brown clay. Attic; late eighth century B.C. Tübingen.

Plate 9. Amphora, painted in brown-black over a white slip. Found in Thera. Cycladic; early seventh century B.C. Ht. $25\frac{3}{4}$ in. Phot. Giraudon. Paris, Bibliothèque Nationale.

During the 'Geometric' period, roughly from 900–700 B.C., Athens and its province of Attica showed greater power of ceramic invention than any other Greek state. Some of the pots, made to stand as monuments over graves, were of great size—four or five feet high, and fitted with a pair of horizontal handles on each side so that two persons could lift them. The Attic potters seem to have thought in terms of large vases, with great areas to be covered with decoration, and as the decorative motives were individually small in extent, they had to be arranged in a semi-architectural manner to help out the vase-shape. Plate 5A shows a successful treatment in the 'strong' geometric manner. Main emphasis was normally given to the zone punctuated by the handles, which formed a horizontal rectangle framed by vertical patterns. Heavier black zones at the bottom of the vase served as ballast for the 'half-tone' hatched ornament higher up; but in later phases the entire surface was often painted in 'half-tone', and careless drawing showed a decline of interest in the geometric designs themselves (1). Stylized animals and birds appeared in the eighth century, and the scene of a dead man on his bier under a canopy, surrounded by male and female mourners, shows how

---

(1) *Plate* 6.

curiously divorced from actual observation was the Greek concept of the human figure at this time (1). The patterns between the mourners are not 'tears'—they are there to fill in the space; and we can safely assume that the jug in Plate 8 comes right at the end of the geometric period both because so much space on it has been left unfilled, and because the 'half-tone' hatched effect of geometric ornament has coagulated into a strong black and white check pattern.

Attic Geometric shapes tended as time went on to lose something of the tightness apparent in the Protogeometric wares, and the plastic snakes on the handles of the Boston amphora (2) suggest that potters had been to some extent lured away from a purely intellectual programme by the sensuous pleasure of manipulating wet clay. The little horses on the circular box are a happy result of their experiments; but nevertheless Attic art generally, including sculpture, has a raw-boned, peasant streak in it from the eighth century till the beginning of the sixth. During this time polish and sophistication was to be found, on the Greek mainland at any rate, in Corinth and the North-East Peloponnese.

It is unnecessary to examine here the numerous other geometric wares of Greece. But some had fine qualities; the big amphora from the island of Thera, for example (3), shows a generous amplitude of shape and a robust indifference to the mania for space-filling that was so pronounced elsewhere—though perhaps these characteristics are partly due to its lateness in date. This vase, like most of those from the Cycladic Islands, is made of a coarse red clay—presumably the only sufficiently plastic material available; the rough surface was covered with a slip of fine white clay to give a good ground for painting.

---

(1) *Plate* 5B; (2) *Plate* 6; (3) *Plate* 9.

The Earliest 'Orientalising' Wares

Plate 10. (*a*) Kotyle, painted in brown-black on greenish buff clay. 'Protocorinthian'; early seventh century B.C. Ht. 3½ in. Boston, Museum of Fine Arts.

Plate 10. (*b*) Krater from Thebes, painted in brown-black on buff clay. 'Protocorinthian'; first half of eighth century B.C. Ht. 8⅞ in. Toronto, Royal Ontario Museum of Archaeology.

Plate 11. (*a*) Pyxis from Phaleron, painted in orange-red on buff clay. 'Protocorinthian'; early seventh century B.C. Diam. 3 in. British Museum.

Plate 11. (*b*) Oinochoe, painted in brown-black on buff clay. 'Protocorinthian'; first half of eighth century B.C. Ht. 9 in. Charles Seltman Collection.

Plate 11. (*c*) Pyxis from Thera. 'Protocorinthian'; first half of eighth century B.C. Ht. 9¼ in. Leyden, Museum of Archaeology.

Plate 12. (*a*) Oinochoe from Corinth. 'Protocorinthian'; second quarter of seventh century B.C. Ht. 4⅞ in. Corinth, American Excavations.

Plate 12. (*b*) Oinochoe, painted in brown-black on brown clay. Probably Rhodian; second quarter of seventh century B.C. Berlin, State Museum.

Plate 13. (*a*) Oinochoe, painted in brown-black. 'Protocorinthian'; about 700 B.C. Würzburg Museum.

Plate 13. (*b*) Aryballos, painted in dark brown on pale buff clay. From Cyme. 'Protocorinthian'; about 700 B.C. Ht. 2⅜ in. Syracuse Museum.

Plate 13. (*c*) Jug from Phaleron. 'Proto-Attic'; second quarter of seventh century B.C. Athens, National Museum.

Plate 14. (*a*) Cover of a pyxis. 'Proto-Attic'; about 700 B.C. Diameter 10¼ in. British Museum.

Plate 14. (*b*) Krater. 'Proto-Attic'; first quarter of seventh century B.C. Munich, Museum Antiker Kleinkunst.

Plate 15. Jug from Aigina. Cycladic Islands; first half of seventh century B.C. Ht. 15¾ in. British Museum.

Corinthian potters lacked imagination in the early Geometric period, but in the eighth century they developed a ware which for technical excellence surpassed anything yet made in the Greek world. They used a fine whitish clay that burnt pale green or buff according to the firing conditions, and a glossy pigment that varied from black to bright orange for the same reason. The so-called 'Protocorinthian' pottery appears at its best in small vessels. As may be seen from the earlier pieces illustrated, the geometric formula was reduced to a scheme of narrow black bands with slight vertical ornament in the main handle-zone. Rarely did there appear a subject so ambitious as the Greek ship on Plate 10B. Living on their Isthmus, the Corinthians were exceptionally well-placed for colonial and trading enterprise both to the east and west, and from the eighth century onwards great quantities of Protocorinthian ware were exported. Local imitations of it were made in many places—for example at Cyme near Naples, the first Greek colony in Italy, founded about 750 B.C.

At Corinth the tradition of geometric ornament on Greek pottery was simplified to the point of bankruptcy. An abstract, introspective art must always play itself out in the end, and it is then time for the artist to raise his eyes and look for fresh inspiration, whether direct from nature or from other people's work. At the end of the eighth century B.C. an easy relationship between art and nature did not exist in any country to which the Greeks had access. But in the East, in Egypt and Assyria, the natural forms of humans, animals, and plants were rendered in a more or less stylized manner with all the assurance of well-matured tradition. Hybrid objects with a composite Oriental flavour were made and peddled by the Phoenicians throughout the Mediterranean; and judging from the finds of Protocorinthian pottery at Poseideion in Syria it now seems likely that Corinth was in almost direct commercial contact with the most civilized areas of Asia. Hence the precocity of Corinth in developing the new style, during the last quarter of the eighth century. Attica was slower to feel the influences of the East; and, paradoxically enough, the Greek cities of Ionia and the Islands were slower still, in spite of their geographical nearness to the Asiatic continent. Asia Minor was culturally backward in comparison with the flatter lands of Syria and Mesopotamia.

There was never any question of the Greeks imitating pottery received from oriental sources. Their own technique was already superior, and the shapes of Greek pottery follow their own natural evolution from the eighth century through the seventh. But it is obvious that the Greek surface-decoration of the seventh century, with its stylized plant forms and animal-friezes, was suggested by eastern art, perhaps through textiles and portable objects of metal, ivory and wood. In almost every case the Greek borrower has so transformed the oriental model to suit his own taste that archaeologists must look in vain for exact correspondences in the East.

The vessels shown in Plates 10–15, so far as they are not purely geometric, are border-line cases where 'orientalising' has just begun. The hatched 'half-tone' effect of geometric painting is giving way; single patterns are allowed to make a good black mark on the vase. For example, the painter of Plate 13A seems overjoyed at his emancipation from drawing thin straight lines. Animals are no longer spiky geometric silhouettes; they have white faces with eyes, and appear capable of convincing movement (1). Plants are still furtive little seedlings (2), sometimes no more than symbols, such as the hooked spiral or the corona of leaf-rays round the base or shoulder of a vase (3). In this intermediary stage between the old geometric build-up and the new scheme of animal-friezes the total decorative composition of a vase is often chaotic, as in the griffon-headed jug from Aigina (4); vestiges of geometric ornament are still found in company with 'black-figure' incised animals (5), and indeed persist beyond the limits of the seventh century. Though 'orientalising' decoration was gradually adopted by one place after another throughout the Greek world, the local character developed by each manufacture during the geometric period usually remained distinct under the veneer of new ornament. Corinthian wares were still neat and precise: Attic potters still played with coils of clay (6). But the animal spout of Plate 12B, and the griffon-head of Plate 15, are something exotic and quite un-Greek; they strongly suggest metallic forms, and may well have been inspired by the brazen cauldrons with zoomorphic handles that reached Greece and even distant Etruria from the foundries near Lake Van in Armenia.

---

(1) *Plates* 13B, 14, 15; (2) *Plate* 13C; (3) *Plates* 12A, 13A, 14B; (4) *Plate* 15; (5) *Plate* 12A; (6) Compare *Plates* 6 and 14B.

East-Greek 'Orientalising' Wares

Plate 16. (*a*) Krateriskos (miniature mixing-bowl), painted in brown-black on buff clay. From Kameiros. Rhodian, second quarter of seventh century B.C. Ht. 6¾ in. British Museum.

Plate 16. (*b*) Fruit-dish on high stand, painted in brown-black with purple and white details, over a white slip. From Kameiros. Rhodian; last quarter of seventh century B.C. Diam. 14¾ in. Phot. Giraudon. Paris, Bibliothèque Nationale.

Plate 17. (*a*) Cup, painted in black and yellow-brown over a white slip. Made in Chios; last quarter of seventh century B.C. Ht. 6⅛ in. Würzburg Museum.

Plate 17. (*b*) Bowl, painted in black, purple and white over white slip. Found at Naukratis in Egypt. Made in Chios; end of seventh century B.C. Diam. 15 in. British Museum.

Plate 18. Oinochoe, painted in black with purple details over a white slip. Perhaps Rhodian; third quarter of seventh century B.C. Ht. 11½ in. Museum of Fine Arts, Boston.

Plate 19. (*a*) Lekythos in form of a duck (spout missing from top of head). From Capua. Painted in brown-black, purple and white on orange clay. East-Greek; third quarter of sixth century B.C. Length 4⅜ in. British Museum.

Plate 19. (*b*) Jar, painted in matt black and red over a dull white slip. Cypriote; perhaps seventh century B.C. Ht. 8⅝ in. Museum of Fine Arts, Boston.

Plate 20. (*a*) Fruit-dish from Rhodes, painted in black, purple and white over white slip, with details incised. Inscribed 'Menelas', 'Euphorbos', 'Hektor' in Argive script. Perhaps Rhodian; first quarter of sixth century B.C. Diam. 15 inches. British Museum.

Plate 20. (*b*) Cup, painted in black and purple on buff clay, with incised outlines. Found in a grave at Ialysos (Rhodes). East-Greek; early sixth century B.C. Diam. 11⅜ in. Rhodes Museum.

Plate 21. (*a*) Kylix with high foot, painted in black and purple on orange clay. East-Greek; mid sixth century B.C. Diam. 9⅜ in. Paris, Louvre.

Plate 21. (*b*) Aryballos (scent-bottle), shaped as a warrior's head. From Kameiros. Painted in black, purple and white on light brown clay, with some engraving. East-Greek; late seventh century B.C. Ht. 2½ in. Oxford, Ashmolean Museum.

Plate 21. (*c*) Aryballos shaped as a gorgon's head. Painted in brown-black, red and white on light brown clay. East-Greek; first half of sixth century B.C. Ht. 2¾ in. Boston, Museum of Fine Arts.

29

Plate 21. (*d*) Aryballos, painted in black, purple and white. East-Greek; first half of sixth century B.C. Ht. 3¾ in. British Museum.

The 'orientalising' style reached rapid maturity during the second and third quarters of the seventh century. A pronounced difference of approach now became apparent in the pottery of Eastern Greece on the one hand, and the Greek mainland on the other. In the East, the favourite material was a somewhat coarse red or buff clay coated with a finer white slip as a ground for painting. The shapes therefore tended to clumsiness in comparison with those of the mainland, where a finer clay, needing no slip, was normally used; and the designs were painted broadly with the brush alone, while on the mainland finer brushwork was gradually superseded by the black-figure silhouette with incised details. Plate 16A illustrates the transition between the stage reached in Plate 12B and the mature 'wild-goat' style (1). The painters aimed at expressing lively movement rather than anatomical structure, yet it is easy to see how the East-Greek birds on the oinochoe Plate 18, could later on take plastic shape (2). It is interesting to compare them with the Cypriote bird (3), which is treated as a purely decorative design that could not under any circumstance become a plastically-organized form. Cyprus lay on the very fringe of the Greek world, and the red-and-black painted ware of which this is an example actually had its forebears in Palestine, in the second millennium B.C. The shape, which assimilates a tripod-stand of metallic origin into the ceramic ensemble of the jar, is likewise derived from Palestinian pottery; though this rather inept feature was also taken up occasionally in Cretan and Attic geometric ware, whether through independent observation of metal pots and stands or through imitating imported Cypriote ware.

Round the base of the oinochoe (4) runs a chain of lotus-flowers and buds—a motive common in Egyptian and Assyrian art. The animals, too, are of Asiatic stock, but the filling-ornaments all round them show a recrudescence, in an acute form, of the peculiarly Greek fear of empty space that we have noticed in the geometric wares. Human figures are of the utmost rarity in early East-Greek painting; there are incised details on the dish (5) which suggests that subject matter, along with technique, had been borrowed from mainland pottery. For all its rich effect, the 'wild-goat' style was of limited range, and in the first half of the sixth century it died out. The latest pieces, conventionally named after the Fikellura cemetery in Rhodes

---

(1) *Plates* 16B, 17, 18; (2) *Plate* 19A; (3) *Plate* 19B; (4) *Plate* 18; (5) *Plate* 20A.

where many were discovered, often show human or animal figures curiously isolated on pots with little other decoration. Local centres of manufacture can be recognized with greater or less certainty in Rhodes, Samos, Chios, Miletus, and Larissa in Aeolis.

Another strain in East Greek ceramics had longer life. Contemporaneously with the later 'wild-goat' wares there were made cups of various shapes in a fine orange-brown clay. Their walls were almost of egg-shell thinness, and a close affinity with engraved metalwork was further suggested by the incised ornament through a black ground, with the addition of purple and white colour (1). Quantities of very fine fragments found at the Greek settlement of Naukratis in Egypt, but known to have been made in Chios, are painted on a white slip ground with human and animal subjects in a surprisingly wide range of colours. About the middle of the sixth century, the pedestal-cup (kylix) became common in East Greece, no doubt following an Attic fashion (2). But the decoration of our example in Plate 21A, with its lively naturalism (3), is quite foreign to mainland art; we may note that the inner lines of the figure are not incised but 'reserved', as in the earlier brush-painted 'wild-goat' wares. The rare surviving fragments show that after this an incised black-figure style of great vitality developed in East Greece; but the best examples of this school are the hydriai found near Caere in Etruria (4).

The sculptural forms, and perhaps even the racial physiognomy, of the Eastern Greeks were tempered by close contact with the Asiatic continent. This may be recognized in the little plastic perfume vases (5).

---

(1) *Plate* 20A; (2) e.g. *Plates* 38B, 39B; (3) Notice the birds' nests with young in the left-hand tree, approached by the mother bird with food, and threatened by a snake. Near by is a cicada sitting on a branch. (4) See p. 43 and *Plates* 58, 59; (5) *Plate* 21.

The Cycladic Islands

Plate 22. Amphora, painted in reddish-brown on pale yellow slip. Cycladic (perhaps made in Paros); middle of seventh century B.C. Ht. 20¾ in. Leyden, Archaeological Museum.

The Islands lying between Asia and the mainland were influenced from both quarters yet developed styles of their own. Big vases were characteristic, and brush painting long remained the favourite technique. The piece illustrated may be compared with its Corinthian contemporary (1) for the tense drawing of the animal, and with its Cycladic predecessors (2) for its 'draughty' openness of composition.

---

(1) *Plate* 23D; (2) *Plates* 9, 15.

A. CORINTHIAN CUP; LAST QUARTER OF 7TH CENTURY B.C.
HT. $5\frac{1}{2}$ IN.
See page 55

Protocorinthian and Corinthian Black-figure

Plate 23. (*a*) Alabastron (scent-bottle). 'Protocorinthian'; about 675 650 B.C. Ht. $2\frac{1}{4}$ in. British Museum.

Plate 23. (*b*) Aryballos (scent-bottle). 'Protocorinthian'; about 675–650 B.C. Ht. $2\frac{9}{16}$ in. Boston, Museum of Fine Arts.

Plate 23. (*c*) The 'Macmillan aryballos' from Thebes. 'Protocorinthian'; about 640 B.C. Ht. $2\frac{5}{8}$ in. British Museum.

Plate 23. (*d*) Kotyle from Kameiros (Rhodes). 'Protocorinthian'; about 675–650 B.C. Ht. $7\frac{1}{2}$ in. British Museum.

Plate 24. (*a*) Oinochoe with 'black polychrome' decoration, from Kameiros. 'Protocorinthian'; about 650–625 B.C. Ht. $8\frac{1}{4}$ in. British Museum.

Plate 24. (*b*) Detail from an olpe, the so-called 'Chigi Vase', found at Veii (Etruria). 'Protocorinthian'; about 640 B.C. Ht. of main frieze, about 2 in. Rome, Villa Giulia.

Plate 25. (*a*) Olpe, from Kameiros (Rhodes). 'Protocorinthian'; about 640–625 B.C. Ht. $7\frac{7}{8}$ in. Oxford, Ashmolean Museum.

Plate 25. (*b*) and (*c*). Aryballos from Kameiros. 'Protocorinthian'; about 640–625 B.C. Ht. $4\frac{15}{16}$ in. British Museum.

Plate 26. (*a*) Scent-bottle in form of an owl, painted in brown-black and purple. 'Protocorinthian'; about 650–625 B.C. Length $2\frac{9}{16}$ in. Paris, Louvre.

Plate 26. (*b*) Aryballos, painted with winged male figure, from Corinth. Corinthian; about 600–575 B.C. Ht. $2\frac{1}{2}$ in. British Museum.

Plate 26. (*c*) Pyxis (covered jar, lid missing). Corinthian; about 580–570 B.C. Oxford, Ashmolean Museum.

Plate 27. (*a*) Fragment of kotyle from Aigina. Protocorinthian; about 650 B.C. Aigina Museum.

Plate 27. (*b*) Cup, from near Corinth. Corinthian; about 570 B.C. Diam. at lip, $7\frac{1}{2}$ in. Boston, Museum of Fine Arts.

Plate 28. (*a*) Cup, from Corinth. Inscribed in Corinthian script with names of Homeric warriors. Corinthian; about 600–575 B.C. Brussels, Bibliothèque Royale.

Plate 28. (*b*) Cup, from Aigina. Corinthian; about 575–550 B.C. Diam. $7\frac{1}{4}$ in. British Museum.

Colour Plate A. Kotyle. Corinthian; last quarter of seventh century B.C. Ht. $3\frac{1}{2}$ in. British Museum.

Plate 37. (*a, b*) Column-krater (and detail) painted in black, white and purple over an orange-red slip. Departure of a bride and groom. From Caere. Corinthian; second quarter of sixth century. Ht. $16\frac{3}{4}$ in. Phot. Alinari. Rome, Vatican.

D

GREEK POTTERY

Fulfilling its earlier promise (1), the 'Protocorinthian' pottery of the half-century 675–625 reached a quite extraordinary refinement of technique. We must look to the Chinese and European porcelain of the eighteenth century A.D. before we can hope to find ceramic objects conceived in quite the same way as the tiny perfume bottles (2). Three friezes—a battle, a horse-race, and a hare-hunt, with thirty-three separate figures—may be packed into a zone less than two inches high (3). Through the base of the little owl-vase (4) runs a hole—it would be carried upside down on a string like an Egyptian scarab; the underside is richly decorated, the orifice of the vase under the tail. On this piece detail is all painted, in black and purple-red on the pale buff Corinthian clay, and brush-painting is found on other examples in the filling-ornament and the tight stylized floral complexes with interlaced bands. But in human and animal figures, which now appear in abundance, the inner structure (and sometimes even the contours) are incised with a sharp point through the dark paint. Experiment has shown that this engraved work can only have been done while the clay was leather-hard, before it went to the kiln. For a century and a half the pot-painters of Corinth and Attica displayed their skill as much through the graving-tool as the brush. In the seventh century this nascent 'black-figure' style was a much brighter, less serious affair than it afterwards became; flesh tones, for example, were often shown in brown-yellow, which with black, purple-red and some white made a comparatively rich colour-scheme. The nape of the hound in Plate 23A was originally painted in yellow and the throat in red over the black; and the scales on Plate 25A showed a similar polychrome effect. But it is for the quality of the engraved line that Protocorinthian ware can claim an admiration almost amounting to awe. From exploring the detail of paw and jowl, it sweeps up round a shoulder with the tension of a bent steel spring; and animals like those on Plates 25B, 27A become monsters more alarming than any in later Greek art. Protocorinthian drawing defines and constructs; with such rare exceptions as the animated hare-hunt on Plate 24B, its movement is an andante with energy held in reserve. Compared with the impressionistic drawing and rapidly diffused movement of seventh-century East-Greek drawing, it reveals a sharp difference of artistic temperament (5).

In the last quarter of the seventh century Corinthian potters were forced to lower their standards of painting to meet the huge demand of foreign markets. Animals were less carefully drawn, with bodies

---

(1) *Plates* 10–13; (2) *Plate* 23; (3) *Plate* 23c; (4) *Plate* 26A; (5) Compare *Plates* 18; 25B, C; 27A.

34

often grotesquely elongated to fill more space. The favourite dot-rosette of 'Protocorinthian' filling ornament becomes in the 'Corinthian' version a solid blob with incised petals, sometimes quite shapeless. But human figures are treated with growing interest and competence; and there is real character in the plastic heads so often associated with the pot-handles (1).

In the first half of the sixth century Attic wares began seriously to compete with Corinthian in the export-trade, and as the warm orange-red Attic clay attracted customers, the Corinthian potters sought to give their own pottery a similar appearance. But the Corinthian clay, being poor in iron, would not burn to a good red; so it had to be covered with a slip containing red ochre. The red-ground Corinthian vases made about 575–50 are remarkable for their showy colours and broadly handled decoration, in which outline brush-painting plays a larger part than in contemporary Attic black-figure (2). But Attic wares eventually secured a virtual monopoly abroad, and from about 550 onwards Corinthian declined into a local industry for home consumption.

---

(1) *Plate* 26c; (2) *Plate* 37.

Lakonian Black-figure

Plate 29. Hydria from Vulci, painted in black and purple over white slip. Lakonian; about 540 B.C. Ht. 15½ in. British Museum.

Plate 30. (*a, b*) Cup, painted in purple and black over white slip. Found at Taranto. Lakonian; about 600 B.C. Taranto, Archaeological Museum.

Plate 31. (*a*) Kylix from Caere, showing Atlas supporting the world, and Prometheus bound. Lakonian; about 550 B.C. Diam. 8 in. Rome, Vatican Museum.

Plate 31. (*b*) Kylix, found at Ialisos in Rhodes. Lakonian; about 600–575 B.C. Diam. 5⅜ in. Rhodes, Archaeological Museum.

Sparta is traditionally known as the archetype of the military state, with a social system of inhuman severity. This idea must be modified in view of archaeological discoveries in Lakonia. Though never in the first rank, Sparta had an art which developed on the same lines as in other Greek states. Its pottery of the seventh and sixth centuries borrowed much from Corinth, but often showed surprising originality —as in the cup full of black and purple fish (1). Mythological subjects were treated in a simple-minded, literal manner that is not un-attractive; notice the pool of gore resulting from the vulture's operations on Prometheus' liver (2). The snake is here a mere filling-ornament. A famous kylix in Paris shows King Arkesilas of Cyrene presiding over the loading of a ship with bales of wool, treated with the most picturesque realism. It is a strange fact that Lakonian wares, though made in small quantity, were very widely exported. Many pieces were found in Samos, others in Italy and Marseilles.

---

(1) *Plate* 30A; (2) *Plate* 31A.

Early Attic Black-figure

Plate 32. Amphora painted in black and purple on deep buff clay. About 625–600 B.C. Ht. 21¾ in. Munich, Museum Antiker Kleinkunst.

Plate 33. (*a*) Olpe, painted in black, purple and white on orange clay, with Hermes between two sphinxes. From Nola. About 600–575 B.C. Ht. 10¼ in. British Museum.

Plate 33. (*b*) Tripod-pyxis, same technique. About 600–575 B.C. Ht. 6⅞ in. Boston, Museum of Fine Arts.

Plate 34. Dinos and stand, same technique. First quarter of sixth century. Total height, 36⅝ in. Phot. Giraudon. Paris, Louvre.

Plate 35. (*a*) Cup, painted in black, white and purple on orange clay, with nude revellers. First quarter of sixth century B.C. Diam. 8¼ in. New York, Metropolitan Museum.

Plate 35. (*b*) Detail from the dinos, Plate 34. Phot. Giraudon.

Plate 36. (*a, b*) Volute-krater from Chiusi (the 'François Vase'), painted in black, purple and white on pale orange clay. Friezes show the Calydonian boar-hunt; the funeral games of Patroklos; the Gods going to the wedding of Thetis; Achilles pursuing Troilos; animals; battle of Pygmies and cranes. Signed 'Ergotimos made me; Klitias painted me'. About 570–565 B.C. Ht. 26 in. Florence, Archaeological Museum.

Plate 38. (*a*) Detail, inside a kylix from Siana (Rhodes). About 575–550 B.C. British Museum.

Plate 38. (*b*) Kylix ('Siana' type), from Rhodes; painted with a priestess at a blazing altar towards which five women dance, pursued by a youth. About 575–550 B.C. Diam. 10½ in. British Museum.

In the National Museum at Athens stands a huge, gaunt sculptured figure, the so-called 'Apollo of Sunium'. It dates from the last quarter of the seventh century. Some contemporary Attic vases in Athens are also huge; their decoration suggests that of Protocorinthian black-figure ware on a giant scale. The amphora in our Plate 32 has the same uncouth vigour, which persists in the chunky drawing on Attic pottery well into the sixth century (1). The clay ground is paler in tone than that of mature Attic 'black-figure', and flesh-tones are commonly shown in broad layers of purple laid over black painting. Quantities of coarsely-made amphorai (the so-called 'Tyrrhenian' or 'Vourva' class) were painted with animal and human friezes and sent to compete in foreign markets with the smaller and more refined

---

(1) *Plates* 33, 34.

Corinthian wares. But already the Athenians were learning to scale down the grossly ornate manner seen, for example, on Plate 34, to suit small vases—particularly cups (1). Ergotimos and Klitias, potter and painter, collaborated to produce the famous krater shown in Plate 36. As a total composition it may lack coherence; but as a manifesto proclaiming the technique and subject-matter of subsequent Attic vase-painting it could not be bettered. Each mythological figure is an individual, labelled by name. The multiple narrative readily finds its way into art when religious or folk traditions are strong and artists unsophisticated: we know from Pausanias about other early Greek examples—the Chest of Kypselos at Corinth, the Throne of Apollo at Amyklai; and in the Gothic art of the Middle Ages they are abundant. However critical, the early Greeks were devout; each city had special patrons among the Gods, and the half-divine Heroes were believed, with some probable basis in fact, to have been actual ancestors of the Greek race. This sense of the divine—$\tau\acute{o}$ $\theta\epsilon\hat{\iota}o\nu$—as a quality that may be reflected in man and his deeds, is a source of profound strength in Greek art and literature until the slow disillusion of the fourth century. The traveller Pausanias, who wrote in the second century A.D., could still recognize it, transfiguring the clumsiness of an early archaic statue at Corinth; and in our study of the humblest Greek pot-painting we should remember that something is present beyond the mere formal activity of the craftsman's hands and mind.

---

(1) *Plate* 35A.

Mature Attic Black-figure

Plate 39. (*a*) Detail, inside a kylix from Vulci, signed 'Tleson, the son of Nearchos made (it)'. Hunter's return. About 550 B.C. British Museum.

Plate 39. (*b*) Kylix (lip-cup) from Vulci, with nonsense inscription. Theseus slaying the Minotaur. Foot replaced by one from a similar kylix. About 550 B.C. Diam. 8⅛ in. British Museum.

Plate 40. (*a*) Detail from cup, Plate 39B.

Plate 40. (*b*) Detail of a cup like Plate 39B, from Naukratis. Odysseus escaping from Polyphemus under a ram. About 550 B.C.

Plate 40. (*c, d*) Kylix from Nola. About 550 B.C. Diam. 8 in. All, British Museum.

Plate 41. (*a, b*) Kylix from Vulci (two views), signed 'Exekias made (it)'. Dionysos sailing. Painted by Exekias, about 540–530 B.C. Diam. 11¾ in. Munich, Museum Antiker Kleinkunst.

Plate 42. Neck-amphora from Vulci. Dionysos and maenads. Signed 'Amasis made me'. Painted by the Amasis-Painter, about 540 B.C. Ht. 12⅝ in. Phot. Giraudon. Paris, Bibliothèque Nationale.

Plate 43. Neck-amphora from Vulci, signed 'Exekias made (it)'. Dionysos and his son Oinopion. Painted by Exekias about 540 B.C. Ht. 16³⁄₁₀ in. British Museum.

Plate 44. Panel-amphora from Vulci, signed 'Exekias painted and made me'. Castor and Pollux return from hunting. About 540–530 B.C. Ht. 31½ in. Phot. Alinari. Rome, Vatican.

Plate 45. (*a*) Detail, reverse of amphora on Plate 44. Achilles and Ajax at dice; Achilles calls 'four', Ajax 'three'.

Plate 45. (*b*) Fragment of a kantharos, from the Acropolis, Athens. Signed 'Nearchos painted me a(nd made me)'. Achilles and his horses, two named Chaitos and Euthyias. About 550 B.C. Athens, National Museum.

Plate 46. Hydria (water-pitcher), showing a portico with five fountain-heads and women fetching water. Three are named Iope, Rhodopis, and Kleo. About 520–500 B.C. Ht. 22⁷⁄₁₀ in. British Museum.

Plate 47. Detail of a hydria from Vulci. Achilles carrying off the dead body of Penthesilea, Queen of the Amazons. About 520 B.C. British Museum.

Plate 48. Amphora. Herakles struggling with Triton. About 540–530 B.C. Phot. Bloesch. Zürich, Technical High School.

Plate 49. (*a*) Detail of Plate 48. Phot. Bloesch.

Plate 49. (*b*) Detail from an amphora. Herakles struggling with the lion of Nemea. By the Andokides Painter. About 530–525 B.C. Phot. Bloesch. Zürich, Technical High School.

Plate 50. Prize amphora ('Panathenaic' shape). Painted with the goddess Athena and inscribed 'From the Games at Athens'. About 500 B.C. Ht. 24½ in. New York, Metropolitan Museum.

Plate 51. Loutrophoros (funeral vase), with no bottom; used as a funnel for pouring libations over the grave. Painted with funeral scenes. About 500 B.C. Ht. 29½ in. New York, Metropolitan Museum.

Plate 52. (*a*) Oinochoe (wine jug), with black-figure painting over white slip. Odysseus escaping under the ram. About 520 B.C. Brussels, Bibliothèque Royale.

Plate 52. (*b*) Plate (pinax) from Vulci. Painted in black-figure on light red clay, by Psiax. Archer in Scythian dress blowing a trumpet. About 520 B.C. Diam. 7½ in. British Museum.

Plate 53. Oinochoe, painted in black-figure over white slip. Probably made by Nikosthenes. About 520 B.C. Brussels, Bibliothèque Royale.

Plate 54. (*a*) Kylix, signed 'Nikosthenes made (it)'. Ships. About 530–520 B.C. Diam. 11 in. Phot. Giraudon. Paris, Louvre.

Plate 55. (*a*) Kyathos (wine-ladle). About 540–520 B.C. Ht. 5⅞ in. Paris, Louvre.

In the generation that followed the painting of the François Vase (1), Athens produced some of the supreme masterpieces of Greek pottery. Large and small vases were treated with equal competence. The tall-stemmed kylix (2) shows a planned unity of form and ornament that for some people can be more exhilarating than anything brought from China. In the best oriental pottery there is always a suggestion of inarticulate growth, like that of a plant; and the seductions of glaze and colour seem half-accidental by-products of a contest between the potter, his materials, and the incalculable element of fire. There is nothing accidental in good Attic pottery; it is the projection upon matter of a vision seen already complete, in a fastidious and essentially masculine mind.

Klitias himself painted some of these 'little-master' cups, and many other painters used their signatures as an integral part of the decoration. Figures are often there as evocative symbols; Odysseus under the ram recalls the ruse by which he and his companions escaped from blind Polyphemus' cave (3); and the ships that nose their way over the unharvested sea, meeting a siren, become part of a story known to every Greek sailor (4). On the larger vases are battle-scenes from *Iliad* or other epics now lost—these poems were often recited at the

---

(1) *Plate* 36; (2) *Plates* 39, 40; (3) *Plate* 40B; (4) *Plate* 54A;

banquets where the pots were used. Achilles plays draughts with Ajax while awaiting the call to battle (1); or he carries off the dead body of the Amazon queen (2). Herakles striving with various monsters offered a welcome alternative to the isolated silhouette figures, and gave opportunity for complicated engraved patterns of interlocking limbs (3). Domestic scenes were only common on the water-jars showing women at the fountain (4); but Dionysos the wine-god, with his attendant silens and maenads, was perhaps the most popular and appropriate subject of all (5).

So much Attic black-figure ware had to be made for export that the painting was often hasty and bad. A broad style was sometimes successful (6), but the greatest masters, Lydos, Nearchos, the Amasis-Painter, and above all, Exekias, aimed rather at enriching their figures with select passages of miraculously fine engraved detail (7). Male flesh was by convention black, female white; purple-red was confined to drapery and accessories. The colour-scheme is deliberately more sombre than that of the early sixth century, when Attic painters, like their Corinthian contemporaries, had made such lavish use of purple; the plant-ornament, too, is less prominent, less fussily engraved. On the François Vase and 'little master' cups, the figures were shown in brisk action. But in the late work of Exekias (8), they appear with greater dignity, in the brooding pause before action has begun, or the moment of relaxation after the hunt is over. Here we have the true climax of the Attic black-figure style.

Exekias' figures are more filled out and massive than those on the François Vase, but it remained for the 'red-figure' painters of the next generation to explore human anatomy in detail, to vary the facial expressions, and to show the folds in drapery. These features were borrowed by the latest black-figure painters, too, for the old technique persisted alongside the new till the end of the sixth century or even later. The amphorai of special shape presented, full of olive oil, to victors in the Panathenaic Games, were still decorated in black-figure at the end of the fourth century (9). The trumpeting archer on Plate 52B is an interesting example of the translation of a red-figure subject back into the black-figure technique (10); no painter brought up in the pure black-figure tradition would so have dared to ignore Greek misgivings about blank space. Similar tendencies appear in the few vases decorated in black-figure on a ground of white slip (11).

---

(1) *Plate* 45A; (2) *Plate* 47; (3) *Plates* 48, 49; (4) *Plate* 46; (5) *Plates* 42, 43; (6) *Plate* 47; (7) *Plates* 43–45; (8) *Plates* 41, 43–45; (9) *Plate* 50; (10) Compare *Plate* 70A; (11) *Plates* 52A, 53.

So-called 'Chalkidian' Wares
(probably Italian-Greek)

Colour Plate. Krater from Vulci. Facing four-horse chariot. About 540 B.C. Ht. 18 in. British Museum.

Plate 54. (*b*) Cup from Vulci. Painted inside with Phineus and the harpies. About 530 B.C. Diam. 15¼ in. Würzburg Museum.

Plate 55. (*b*) Cup. About 530 B.C. Foot restored. New York, Metropolitan Museum.

Plate 56. Neck-amphora, showing the three-bodied monster Geryones in combat with Herakles. Eurytion lies dead. About 540–530 B.C. Ht. 16⅛ in. Phot. Giraudon. Paris, Bibliothèque Nationale.

Plate 57. Hydria from Vulci. About 540–530 B.C. Ht. 10¼ in. Cambridge, Fitzwilliam Museum.

A series of black-figure wares found only in Southern Italy and Sicily bear inscriptions in the peculiar lettering used in Euboea, the long island east of Attica. Chalkis in Euboea was formerly suggested as the home of this manufacture, which lasted from about 560–520 B.C. But the distribution of finds, and certain resemblances to native Italian wares, indicate that the 'Chalkidian' vases were made by Euboean settlers in South Italy. Technically they are very good and very like Attic black-figure. Shapes and figure-subjects were to some extent borrowed from Corinthian red-ground and Attic wares; but the drawing has its own broad and robust style. Painted inside the Würzburg cup (1) is a badly damaged frieze showing Phineus molested at his dinner by Harpies. The figures here have a fulsome roundness shared also by the exterior ornament; due, no doubt, to that wave of 'Ionian' or East-Greek taste that also became evident in Attica between about 540 and 520 B.C. The Euboeans were of Ionian stock, and this element was strong in the Greek-Italian colonies. Eyes painted on Greek pots (and ships) are explained as averters of evil. They are at any rate good decoration. The high handles of 'Chalkidian' cups, rising above rim-level, would prevent their being easily hung face inwards against a wall. Attic cup-handles are more practical, and usually curve flush with the rim or slightly below it (2). Nor did 'Chalkidian' potters so fully appreciate the aesthetic value of a break in the main frieze below the handle on an amphora (see page 15, note 1).

---

(1) *Plate* 54B; (2) *Plates* 39, 40, 41, 74, 75.

B. 'CHALKIDIAN' MIXING-BOWL; ABOUT 540 B.C. HT. 18 IN.
See page 42

Late East-Greek Black-figure

Plate 58. Hydria from Italy, painted in black, red and white on orange clay, with the hunting of the Calydonian boar. So-called 'Caeretan' class; about 540–530 B.C. Ht. 17¼ in. Phot. Giraudon. Paris, Louvre.

Plate 59. Hydria, technique as last. From Italy. So-called 'Caeretan' class; about 540–530 B.C. Ht. 17¾ in. Phot. Giraudon. Paris, Louvre.

Plate 60. (*a*) Scent-bottle in the form of a girl. Traces of red paint on dress. East-Greek; about 540 B.C. Ht. 5¼ in. British Museum.

Plate 60. (*b*) Detail from a hydria of the so-called 'Caeretan' class. Hunted lioness at bay. Paris, Louvre.

Plate 61. Alabastron (perfume bottle) in the form of a boy. Found in the Agora at Athens. East-Greek or Attic; about 540–530 B.C. Ht. 10 in. Athens, National Museum.

In the middle and second half of the sixth century the Greek cities of Asia Minor found their independence threatened by strongly organized Asiatic powers. First Croesus of Lydia, then Cyrus and Darius the Great of Persia bore heavily on them; East Greek civilization was eclipsed in the events that preceded the two Persian invasions of Mainland Greece at the beginning of the fifth century. As early as about 540 B.C. the citizens of Phocaea abandoned their city in Asia for new homes in the west.

Craftsmen from Eastern Greece seem to have fled early from the coming storm. One, a potter, apparently settled in Italy: the twenty-five odd vases or fragments from his hand were discovered round Caere and Vulci in Etruria. Almost all are hydriai of fine orange or brown clay. Their full, rounded forms are painted with robust plant ornament, and with incised black-figure subjects. This East-Greek style stands in marked contrast to the dry fastidiousness of Attic black-figure. There is much colour, purple being often laid direct on the clay; well-observed naturalism in animals and plants; energetic movement in the fleshy human figures; and great freedom and delicacy in the incised lines, which differ from Attic lines in the same way as etching differs from copper-engraving. Where in East-Greece the maker of the 'Caeretan' hydriai learnt his art is unknown; he belonged to the generation after the cup in Plate 21A was painted, and sites in the Eastern Mediterranean area have yielded only a few Ionian black-figure vases or fragments of comparable excellence.

Persons like those painted on the 'Caeretan' vases appear also in plastic form. The scent-bottle moulded to represent a half-length figure of a maiden holding a dove is certainly East-Greek (1); but the kneeling boy, for all his Eastern appearance, might possibly have been made in Athens at a time when 'Ionian' taste was becoming fashionable there (2). He originally held a gold or silver wreath in his raised hands, ready to bind it round his head—the groove through which it passed is just under the bottle-neck. The head and body are hollow-moulded, the arms and legs solid, and modelled by hand. The hair was painted red. This is the finest Greek pottery figure known, and ranks with the best archaic sculpture; only from a full series of photographs or from the original itself can one appreciate the exquisite counterplay between naturalism and firm stylization, between the soft flesh and suggested bone.

Early Attic Red-figure

Plate 62. (*a*, *b*) Stamnos (wine-jar) from Cervetri. Herakles in combat with the river-god Acheloös. Signed 'Pamphaios made (it)'; painted by Oltos. About 525 B.C. Ht. 10⅞ in. British Museum.
Plate 63. (*a*) Cup, with one flat tilted handle. Dancers. Perhaps painted by Psiax. About 525 B.C. 5½ in. Victoria and Albert Museum.
Plate 63. (*b*) Detail of a panel-amphora from Vulci. Herakles and Apollo struggling for the Tripod of Delphi. Signed 'Andokides made (it)'. By the Andokides Painter. About 530–525 B.C. Berlin, State Museum.
Plate 64. Amphora, modified from a metallic shape favoured by the potter Nikosthenes. Silen and maenad; girl putting on shoe. Signed 'Pamphaios made (it)'; painted by Oltos. About 525–520 B.C. Ht. 14¾ in. Paris, Louvre.

The Attic red-figure style may have been suggested by changes in contemporary wall-painting. Figures were first roughly sketched on the dried pot with a blunt tool, and then defined by a guiding-line in some fugitive pigment that would show through the wash of slip and potash that was next applied (see page 5). Then, using the concentrated wash that produced the black colour, the artist carefully drew a band about one-eighth of an inch wide round the outside of the guiding-line; and proceeded to indicate with fine, painted 'relief-lines' those inner details of anatomy and drapery that on black-figure wares had been shown by engraving. The 'relief-lines' are long, steady strokes; they have an almost metallic springiness. Human hair was sometimes done in piled-up spots of black to represent curls, or partly in black and partly in the same pigment thinned to produce a golden brown; it was marked off from the black background where necessary by an incised or reserved line. Muscles and hair on the body were often shown in the same golden brown 'diluted' pigment. When the figures and ornament had been painted, it was left for the artist to fill in the black background. Inscriptions were often painted on this background in purple, and touches of the same colour were used sparingly on the hair-bands or other accessories of the figures themselves. White painting was very rare.

The red-figure style was invented between 530–520 B.C., probably by one of the painters who worked for the potter Andokides. He had been a pupil of Exekias, had done much black-figure work (1); some-

---

(1) e.g. *Plate* 49B.

times he combined both techniques, on the two sides of a single vase. His copiously patterned draperies are like those of Exekias, but show folds; in his figures massiveness of bone and muscle has become a somewhat epicene plumpness of flesh; and the receding profiles suggest those of East-Greek art. About this time Ionian fashions were prevalent in Athens; instead of the 'peplos', a single garment of thick material, women were adopting the thin, rippling Ionian 'chiton' with a cloak slung obliquely over it. This dress allowed the artist great opportunities for making complex patterns from the falling folds, as may be seen in the marble statues of maidens dedicated on the Acropolis, and in Attic vase-painting generally during the last quarter of the sixth century. But the Andokides painter and his more virile contemporary Oltos stand only at the beginning of this ornate phase in Attic art.

Attica; Late Archaic Red-figure

Plate 65. Panel-amphora from Vulci. Theseus carrying off Korone. Painted by Euthymides. About 510–500 B.C. Ht. $23\frac{5}{8}$ in. Munich, Museum Antiker Kleinkunst.

Plate 66. (*a*) Maenad, detail from Plate 67.

Plate 66. (*b*) Theseus and Korone, detail from Plate 65.

Plate 67. Amphora, to stand in a ring-support. Dionysos and maenads. By the Kleophrades Painter. About 500–490 B.C. Ht. $22\frac{1}{16}$ in. Munich, Museum Antiker Kleinkunst.

Plate 68. (*a*) Calyx-krater. Athletes. Painted by Euphronios. About 500 B.C. Ht. $13\frac{13}{16}$ in. Berlin, State Museum.

Plate 68. (*b*) Detail from a calyx-krater, painted by Euphronios. Herakles struggling with Antaios. About 500 B.C. Paris, Louvre.

Plate 69. (*a* and *b*) Kotyle from Capua. Triptolemos in a winged car; behind him Demeter, goddess of harvest. Signed 'Hieron made (it)'; painted by Makron. About 500–490 B.C. Ht. $8\frac{1}{4}$ in. British Museum.

Colour Plate C. Kylix from Vulci, shown as if hanging against a wall. Theseus slaying the Minotaur; revellers. Signed 'Epiktetos painted (it)'. About 520 B.C. Diam. $11\frac{5}{8}$ in. British Museum.

Plate 70. (*a*) Plate from Vulci. Archer in Scythian dress. Signed 'Epiktetos painted (it)'. About 520 B.C. Diam. $7\frac{5}{8}$ in.

Plate 70. (*b*) Detail of kylix from Vulci. Sleep and Death with the body of Sarpedon. Signed 'Pamphaios made (it)'; perhaps painted by the Nikosthenes Painter. About 510 B.C. Both, British Museum.

Plate 71. (*a*) Detail inside a kylix from Vulci. Flute player and dancer. Signed 'Python made (it); Epiktetos painted (it)'. About 520–510 B.C.

Plate 71. (*b*) Detail, exterior of last. Herakles slaying Busiris, King of Egypt. British Museum.

Plate 72. (*a*) Detail, inside a kylix from Orvieto. Silen on amphora. By the Panaitios Painter. About 510–500 B.C. Boston, Museum of Fine Arts.

Plate 72. (*b*) Detail, outside a kylix from Vulci. Whole scene shows Herakles, the Erymanthian boar, and Eurystheus. By the Panaitios Painter. British Museum. About 500 B.C.

Plate 73. (*a*) Detail, inside a kylix from Vulci. Amazons charging, named Hippolyte and Thero. Manner of the Panaitios Painter. About 520–510 B.C.

Plate 73. (*b*) Exterior of last. Amazons to the rescue of Hippolyte, who has been downed by Herakles. British Museum.

Plate 74. (*a*) Detail of cup below. Hera pursued by silens; Hermes and Herakles.

Plate 74. (*b*) Kylix from Capua. Signed 'Brygos made (it)'; by the Brygos Painter. About 490–480 B.C. Ht. 4⅞ in. Diam. 10¹³⁄₁₆ in. British Museum.

Plate 75. (*a*) Kylix from Vulci. Revellers. Signed 'Brygos made (it)'; by the Brygos Painter. About 490–480 B.C. Diam. 12⁵⁄₁₆ in. Würzburg Museum.

Plate 75. (*b*) Kylix from Vulci. By the Brygos Painter. About 490–480 B.C. Ht. 5 in. Diam. 12⅝ in. British Museum.

Plate 76. (*a*) Kantharos from Thebes. Zeus pursuing Ganymede. By the Brygos Painter. About 490–480 B.C. Ht. 9½ in. Boston, Museum of Fine Arts.

Plate 76. (*b*) Box from Aigina, shaped like a knuckle-bone, probably to contain real knuckle-bones for the game. Hephaistos, whose forge is imagined inside the cavern, gathers the clouds, shown as maidens; a burlesque on Homer's Zeus the Cloud-gatherer (νεφεληγερέτα Ζεύς). Painted by Sotades about 470–460 B.C. Length 6 in. British Museum.

Plate 77. Cooler (psykter) to be filled with ice or water and lowered into a wine-krater. From Cervetri. Drunken silens, one pouring from a wine-skin. Signed 'Douris painted (it)'. About 480–470 B.C. Ht. 11¼ in. British Museum.

Plate 78. Volute-krater, from Caere. Achilles slays Hektor. By the Berlin Painter. About 480 B.C. Ht. 25¾ in. British Museum.

Plate 79. Amphora from Vulci. Herakles with the Tripod (Apollo on the reverse). By the Berlin Painter. About 490–480 B.C. Ht. 20¾ in. Würzburg Museum.

The term 'classical', as applied to Greek art or any other, is properly used to denote a phase when the artist has attained effortless control of his medium, and uses it to suggest a spiritual harmony whose amplitude lies beyond the world of ordinary experience. The classical mood was foreshadowed in the vase-painting of Exekias (1); by the middle of the fifth century it pervaded Greek art as a whole. And in consequence something perhaps more valuable was lost. Late archaic vase-painting still shows the passion of adolescence, a humanity too restless and vital, too absorbed in action to affect the dignity of gods. One is constantly reminded of Italian quattrocento painting. Euphronios, like Pollaiuolo, understood the anguish of physical combat (2); the Kleophrades Painter gave his frenzied Maenad the massive truculence of Signorelli's damned (3). In his innocent drawing Epiktetos is akin to Pisanello, another master of circular composition (4). The Greek artists, like the Italians, were much occupied with

---

(1) *Plates* 41, 43–45; (2) *Plate* 68B; (3) *Plate* 66A; (4) *Plates* 70, 71.

C. ATTIC CUP SIGNED BY THE PAINTER EPIKTETOS;
ABOUT 520 B.C. DIAM. $11\frac{5}{8}$ IN.
See page 47

anatomy and foreshortening; they delighted in a lavishly decorative treatment of drapery. But these analogies should not be pressed too far. We may more aptly compare the cheerful tone of red-figure painting with that of its predecessor. Black-figure battles were grim; now they often resemble a high-spirited dance (1). There is rich caricature in the Silen (2), who seems to hold ready an appropriate answer to Roger Fry's criticism that this vein is lacking in Greek art. A religious subject is handled with radiant felicity (3); a Homeric scene with a new kind of pathos (4). Most remarkable is the increased popularity of scenes from daily life, from school, from the gymnasium, from the roaring excesses of the drinking party (5).

The different moods of the painting correspond to the temperaments of individual artists; the rapidly developing skill in drawing anatomy was largely based on collective knowledge. Some painters signed their work—'Epiktetos painted (it)'; the formula 'Euphronios made (it)' means that the pot was produced in the factory owned by Euphronios and painted by one of the many artists who worked for him (6). Sometimes the master both 'made and painted' the vase himself—Euthymides once adds 'better than Euphronios could ever have done'. We know from the re-combination of inscriptions that painters might move from one factory to another. Professor Beazley has been able to distinguish the style of some five hundred different painters, and there are cases where over two hundred pieces painted by a single man have survived. Most of these artists are anonymous, and for convenience they have been named after subjects or inscriptions on their work, or after the collections in which their work is represented.

Many vase-shapes current in the black-figure period persisted when the style of painting changed. But there are important modifications, as may be seen by comparing the typical red-figure kylix with its predecessors (7). The base of these wide cups is to be regarded as a third handle rather than a stand, for when not in use the cup would be suspended by one of the side-handles from a nail in the wall (8). The decoration, too, is intended to be read as the cup is turned in the hand. Other shapes show a comparable unification of outline into a suaver

---

(1) *Plate* 73B; (2) *Plate* 72A; (3) *Plate* 69; (4) *Plate* 70B; (5) *Plates* 68A, 75A; (6) Note: This has till recently been the accepted view. But Professor Beazley and Dr. Bloesch, whose opinions deserve the highest respect, now incline to believe that the master-potter did in fact 'make' the pot with his own hands. If this was so, the Greeks obviously considered the 'making' (i.e. the shape) of the pot more important than the decoration; (7) *Plates* 75, 38–41, 54A; (8) *Colour Plate C.*

curve—for example, the hydria (1) and the new pelike-amphora (2). The new neck-amphora, of which many examples were found at Nola in South Italy, is slighter and more elegant than the black-figure version (3).

The composition of the painting in relation to the space continues the black-figure tradition, though the new technique allows more overlapping of figures and limbs. In some pieces painted by Euphronios the grouping is almost too elaborate—one feels that he above others is conscious of the developments in contemporary wall-painting. Perhaps the most gifted of all is the Brygos Painter, who on the outside of a kylix can vividly suggest the unsteadiness of a drunken rout (4), or introduce violent cross-rhythms that bind a group of figures together in psychological as well as formal tension (5).

---

(1) *Plates* 81 and 46; (2) *Plate* 84; (3) *Plates* 80, 42, 43; (4) *Plate* 75A; (5) *Plates* 74A, 76A.

Attic 'Classical' Vases

Plate 80. Amphora of 'Nolan' shape, painted by the Phiale-Painter. About 440 B.C. Ht. 13½ in. Victoria and Albert Museum.

Plate 81. Hydria. Boreas carries off Orithyia. About 470–460 B.C. Ht. 15½ in. Victoria and Albert Museum.

Plates 82, 83. Bell-krater from Cumae. Artemis slays Actaeon, who had molested Semele. By the Pan-Painter. About 470–460 B.C. Ht. 14¾ in. Boston, Museum of Fine Arts.

Plate 84. Pelike from Boeotia. Herakles slays Busiris, King of Egypt. By the Pan-Painter. About 470–460 B.C. Ht. 12$\frac{3}{16}$ in. Athens, National Museum.

Plate 85. Detail of amphora from Vulci. Achilles. By the Achilles-Painter. About 450 B.C. Rome, Vatican.

Plate 86. Detail of amphora from Vulci. Terpsichore, with Mousaios and Melousa. By the Peleus-Painter. About 450 B.C. British Museum.

Plate 87. Calyx-krater from Orvieto. Apollo and Artemis slay the children of Niobe. By the Niobid-Painter. About 460–450 B.C. Ht. 21¼ in. Paris, Louvre.

It was the generation of artists working between 480 and 450 B.C. that created the 'Classical type' of humanity, in which an uniform conception of ideal beauty replaced the livelier characterization of individual differences. We can still see great sculpture of this time at Olympia, but nothing remains of the celebrated frescoes in public buildings of Athens and Delphi painted by Polygnotus the Thasian. It was difficult for vase-painters working on a miniature scale to adapt themselves to the new ideas of grandeur. Some did not try. The Pan-Painter deliberately prolonged the life of the archaic style; yet for all their animation his long-limbed figures contrive an elegance that is slightly mannered, and the death of Actaeon becomes the arabesque of a graceful ballet (1). By a curious accident the turning figure of Artemis here suggests the *figura serpentinata* so dear to 'mannerist' sculptors of the sixteenth century. Other vase-painters imitated wall-painting with disastrous results; either huge figures overcrowded the frieze; or the frieze arrangement was abandoned for a kind of uphill perspective like that of a Persian miniature (2). We know from Pausanias' description of frescoes at Delphi that this convention was used by the wall-painter Polygnotus, of whose style this vase is a convincing record. A third sequence of vase-painters approached the

---

(1) *Plates* 82, 83; (2) *Plate* 87.

classical style with more prudence. Perhaps as early as 480 B.C. certain shapes were appropriately decorated with a single figure, or pair of figures, standing isolated on a completely black background (1). This scheme suited the Achilles-Painter; our Plate 85, painted about 450 B.C., shows his noble rendering of a 'classical' hero on an amphora among the best of the 'classical' vases. The Achilles-Painter remained true to the profile treatment of the head on his many white-ground vases (see p. 53); but a contemporary at last adopted the fatal three-quarter view (2), and we notice a new character in the drawn relief-lines. They have lost the springiness of archaic drawing, and aim at the same effect of softly flowing drapery as the Parthenon sculptures. Along this path vase-painting was to make its rapid descent to the bathos and triviality of the Meidias-Painter (p. 57).

Attic White-ground Vases

Colour Plate D. Kylix from Kameiros (Rhodes). Aphrodite riding on a goose. By the Pistoxenos-Painter. About 465 B.C. Diam. $9\frac{1}{2}$ in. British Museum.

Plate 88. (*a*) Oinochoe, painted in outline and colours. About 475 B.C. Athens, National Museum.

Plate 88. (*b*) Turned cups (phiale and mastos), painted in purple, white and black. The phiale signed 'Sotades made (it)'. About 475–460 B.C. Diam. of phiale $6\frac{5}{8}$ in. Ht. of mastos, $3\frac{1}{4}$ in. British Museum.

Plate 89. (*a*). Alabastron painted in black. About 500 B.C. Ht. 5 in. New York, Metropolitan Museum.

Plate 89. (*b*) Painted in brown-black. From Tanagra. About 500 B.C. Ht. $6\frac{3}{8}$ in.

Plate 89. (*c*) Painted in black, yellow-brown, and red. From Marion, Cyprus. Signed 'Pasiades made (it)'. About 500 B.C. Ht. $5\frac{3}{4}$ in. British Museum.

Plate 89. (*d*) Kylix from Vulci, painted in black, yellow-brown and red. Maenad. By the Brygos-Painter. About 490–480 B.C. Munich, Museum Antiker Kleinkunst.

Plate 90. (*a*) Funeral lekythos, painted in black, opaque white, and two shades of purple-red. About 470 B.C. Ht. 14 in.

Plate 90. (*b*) Funeral lekythos from Cyprus, painted in brown, black and red. Warrior arming. By the Achilles-Painter. About 450 B.C. Ht. $15\frac{1}{2}$ in. Both, British Museum.

Plate 91. (*a*) Pyxis from Cumae, painted in black, yellow-brown and purple. The Judgment of Paris. By the Penthesilea-Painter. About 465 B.C. Ht. $6\frac{3}{4}$ in. New York, Metropolitan Museum.

Plate 91. (*b*) Flattened-out photograph of painting on a lekythos, like Plate 90B. Soldier's farewell. By the Achilles-Painter. About 450–440 B.C. Athens, National Museum.

Most white-ground Attic vases of the late sixth century formed a mere sub-species of Attic black-figure (1), and the little scent-bottle in Plate 89A is one of them. But its companion, Plate 89C, shows the beginning of a distinct white-ground style, with figures drawn in outline. Red-figure painters occasionally did cups in this way; outlines in black, inner lines in golden brown, the white slip covered with a very dilute wash of the painting-mixture to give it a smooth, ivory-toned surface. One man specialized in painting negroes and Amazons

---

(1) See also *Plates* 52A, 53, p. 40.

with very unusual breadth (1). In the second quarter of the fifth century quite a number of cups, toilet-boxes and so on were painted in black or golden-brown outline, with areas colour-washed in purple, red, and yellow ochre; their attractiveness is enhanced by peculiarly sensitive drawing (2). But the white slip was easily chipped or abraded, and the technique was mainly reserved for vases of a special kind, the lekythoi that were buried with the dead or offered on their tombs (3). This shape had been long in general use as an oil-bottle before its dedication to funeral purposes in the second quarter of the fifth century. The Achilles-Painter, who also worked in red-figure (p. 52), has left a long series of white-ground lekythoi, and his restrained classical style is here well in keeping. The figures make no parade of grief, but their gravity conveys its overtone; the girl adorning herself, the young man shown arming on the vase, is now dead. Sometimes he stands, as in life, beside the tomb where wife or sister lay their offerings. Later painters showed the dead ones, men or women, preparing for their last journey across the Styx; Charon waits, with unkempt hair and shaggy coat, holding his boat to the bank. These funeral vases were still made during the Peloponnesian War, till the end of the fifth century; inferior in technique to those by the Achilles-Painter, though more variously coloured, their free, sketchy drawing suggests a mood of wilder tragedy.

---

(1) *Plate* 89B; (2) *Colour Plate D: Plates* 88A, 91A; (3) *Plates* 90, 91B.

D. ATTIC CUP, BY THE PISTOXENOS PAINTER; ABOUT 465 B.C.

DIAM. $9\frac{1}{2}$ IN.

See page 55

Plastic Vases, etc.

Plate 92. (*a*) Negro-head vase, painted in black with white eyeballs, the rest bare orange-red clay. Attic, about 500 B.C. Ht. 5½ in. British Museum.

Plate 92. (*b*) Cup in form of a woman's head, painted in black with white eyeballs, the rest bare orange-red clay. Attic; about 500–490 B.C. Ht. 7⅜ in. New York, Metropolitan Museum.

Plate 92. (*c*) Cup from Capua, in form of ram's head. Painted by the Syriskos-Painter in black, red and white, with much bare orange-red clay. Attic; about 500–490 B.C. Length 8¼ in. British Museum.

Plate 93. (*a*) Terra-cotta figure from Eretria (Euboea), originally painted in matt-white, brownish-red, blue and pink. Probably made at Tanagra in Boeotia; late fourth or third century B.C. Ht. 9 in. British Museum.

'Plastic' vases were always a side-line with Greek potters, a kind of joke (1). They are best when the subject is itself grotesque—the negro's head and the ram are excellently modelled and full of humour. The numerous cups in the shape of a girl's head are usually more insipid, perhaps because one feels called on to compare them with serious sculpture. Sometimes the heads of a girl and a negro, or a maenad and a silen, are joined back to back in a single cup. It is not a happy idea to combine a plastic head with a vase-mouth painted in the normal way with figures on a smaller scale. And the fifth-century vases in the too humanly female form of a sphinx are among the most repellent artifacts of all time. All these plastic vases were moulded in two separate halves subsequently joined down the sides of the head (human) or down the middle (animal). Such things, like Toby-jugs, can be amusing in moderation, and the Athenians were sufficiently amused to support at least one fun-specialist among the potters of each generation.

Misplaced admiration has been directed upon the ornamental terra-cotta figurines made in Hellenistic times at Tanagra in Boeotia, at Smyrna, Myrrhina and various other places. They usually represent young women of light calibre pulling their dresses into pretty patterns; or *erotes* (cupids) in a condition of adolescent and epicene nudity. Connoisseurs of such things generally prefer the numerous modern fakes, which are specially sweetened in the manner required.

---

(1) Earlier examples are shown on *Plates* 21, 26, 60 and 61.

GREEK POTTERY

The genuine figure in Plate 93A is better than most. Normally the modelling is more faded and feeble, for after all the material was rather coarse. In spite of a certain felicity of pose, these figures quite lack the vitality and wit often seen in porcelain figures of the eighteenth century.

The Decline of Greek Vase-painting

Plate 93. (*b*) Detail, cover of toilet-box. Women and erotes (cupids). Red-figure technique with raised points for gilding. By the Meidias-Painter. Attic; late fifth century B.C. Oxford, Ashmolean Museum.

Plate 94. (*a*) Hydria, signed 'Meidias made (it)'; by the Meidias-Painter. Above, Castor and Pollux carry off the daughters of Leukippos; below, Herakles in the Garden of the Hesperides; Attic heroes, etc. Red-figure technique with gilding. Attic; late fifth century B.C. Ht. 20½ in. British Museum.

Plate 94. (*b*) Toilet-box (pyxis), with red-figure painting. Apollo. Attic; early fourth century B.C. Diam. 2$\frac{11}{16}$. Oxford, Ashmolean Museum.

Plate 95. (*a*) Toy cup from Tanagra, for playing 'kottabos' (splash and sink the dummy duck). Painted in brown-black and purple on buff clay. Boeotian; fourth century B.C. Diam. 3½ in. British Museum.

Plate 95. (*b*) So-called 'Megarian bowl'; third-second century B.C. Diam. 4$\frac{5}{8}$ in. British Museum.

Plate 96. Hydria. Attic; about 350 B.C. Ht. 21¼ in. Phot. Bloesch. Winterthur, Art Museum.

From the early Iron Age till the middle of the fifth century B.C. pottery meant more to the Greeks than to most other peoples before or since; it was an adequate means for expressing the best creative ideas of Greek art. Then, quite suddenly, interest turned elsewhere—to the large paintings on wall or panel, to plastic and spatial realism beyond the vase-painter's scope. Even in major art the 'classical' reconciliation of grace with strength could not last; strength broke away, turbulent and demonstrative; grace alone became over-sweet; and the 'classical type' of humanity saddled the minor artist with a collection of lay figures that he was unable to reanimate. The Meidias-Painter, like other red-figure artists of the last quarter of the fifth century, singled out from the mature classical art of the Parthenon just those florid elements that could be developed towards over-sweetness. In decorating a large vase (1) he discarded all the precariously integrated architecture of shape and painted design that earlier potters had thought so important. He was happier painting small toilet-boxes and the like (2); covering them with plump little trollops in gauze, *Eldorado banal de tous les vieux garçons.*

---

(1) *Plate* 94A; (2) *Plate* 93B.

Athens was defeated by Sparta and her allies in the Peloponnesian War, which ended in 404 B.C. It cannot have been a propitious time for the arts. For a short while at the beginning of the fourth century an attempt was made to revive Attic red-figure vase-painting in an extremely florid style; many examples have been found at Kertch in the Crimea. And Attic potters who settled in South Italy about 440 founded a school of red-figure painting whose off-shoots remained active till the third century B.C. But it would be depressing to explore further. In Athens and the Eastern Mediterranean generally it was felt that the days of painted pottery as an art were over. The most characteristic pottery of the fourth century and of Hellenistic times frankly borrowed its shapes and its moulded relief-ornament from metal vases, and thereby sometimes acquired an attenuated elegance (I). With their shiny coat of uniform black or red colouring, such wares can only have been regarded as cheap substitutes for bronze. The red *terra sigillata* made especially at Arezzo and various places in Gaul continued the same tradition in Roman times.

(I) *Plate* 96.

SHORT BIBLIOGRAPHY

(The following works are selected either because they can be easily read by the non-specialist, or because they contain exceptionally good or extensive illustrations. Among the volumes of the fully illustrated *Corpus Vasorum Antiquorum*, those for the Ashmolean Museum, Oxford, and Fitzwilliam Museum, Cambridge, are particularly well produced; the volumes for the British Museum and the Louvre are the richest in material.)

Beazley, J. D. *Attic red-figured vases in American Museums* (Cambridge, Mass., 1918).

    Attic black-figure; a sketch (London, 1928).

    Greek Vases in Poland (Oxford, 1928).

    Der Berliner Maler (Berlin, 1930).

    Der Pan-Maler (Berlin, 1930).

    Der Kleophrades-Maler (Berlin, 1933).

    Attic white lekythoi (London, 1938).

Beazley, J. D., and Ashmole, B. *Greek sculpture and painting* (Cambridge, 1932).

Bossert, H. T. *The Art of Ancient Crete* (London, 1937).

Buschor, E. (transl. G. L. Richards.) *Greek vase-painting* (London, 1921).

Cook, R. M. *Greek painted pottery* (in preparation).

Daremberg, C., and Saglio, E. *Dictionnaire des antiquités grecques et romaines*, 1912–17, article Vasa, by Ch. Dugas.

Dennis, G. *The cities and cemeteries of Etruria* (London, 1848, and later editions).

Encyclopédie photographique de l'art. Musée du Louvre II, III (Editions Tel, Paris, 1936, 1938).

Fairbanks, A. *Athenian lekythoi with outline drawing* (New York, 1907 and 1914).

    Catalogue of Greek & Etruscan vases in the Museum of Fine Arts, Boston (Cambridge, Mass., 1928).

Fürtwangler, A. and Reichhold, K., with others. *Griechische Vasenmalerei*. Munich, 1904–22. (Full-scale drawings.)

Hoppin, J. C. *A handbook of Attic red-figured vases* (Cambridge, Mass., 1919).

    A handbook of Attic black-figured vases (Paris, 1924).

GREEK POTTERY

Jakobstahl, P. *Ornamente griechischer Vasen* (Berlin, 1927).

Johansen, K. Friis. *Les vases sicyoniens* (Paris and Copenhagen, 1923) (about Protocorinthian).

Payne, H. *Necrocorinthia; a study of Corinthian art in the archaic period* (Oxford, 1931). (Protocorinthian, Corinthian, and Attic black-figure.)

　　Protokorintische Vasen (Berlin, 1933).

Pfuhl, E. *Malerei und Zeichnung der Griechen* (Munich, 1923).

　　(Transl. Beazley). *Masterpieces of Greek drawing and painting* (London, 1926).

Richter, G. M. A. *The craft of Athenian pottery* (New Haven, 1923).

Richter, G. M. A. and Milne, M. J. *Shapes and names of Athenian vases* (New York, 1935).

　　Attic red-figured vases (New Haven, 1946).

Riezler, W. *Weissgrundige attische Lekythen* (Munich, 1914).

Rumpf, A. *Chalkidische Vasen* (Berlin & Leipzig, 1927).

Seltman, C. *Attic vase-painting* (Cambridge, Mass., 1933).

Swindler, A. H. *Ancient painting* (New Haven, 1929).

Technau, W. *Exekias* (Berlin, 1936).

Walters, H. B. *History of ancient pottery* (London, 1905).

Zervos, C. *L'art en Grèce* (Paris, 1934).

INDEX

61

INDEX

PLATES

PLATES

1. CRETE ('LATE MINOAN I'). ABOUT 1550–1450 B.C. HT. $9\frac{7}{8}$ IN.
See page 22

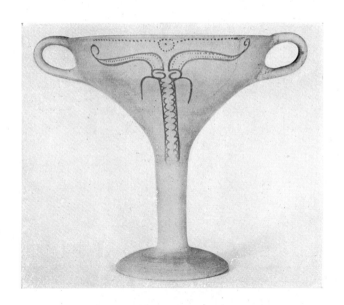

2A. 'LATE HELLADIC III'. ABOUT 1375–1200 B.C.
FROM KALYMNOS, HT. 7½ IN.
2B. 'LATE HELLADIC III'; ABOUT 1375–1200 B.C.
FROM CYPRUS, HT. 10½ IN.
See page 22

3A. ATTIC ('PROTOGEOMETRIC'). ABOUT 1000–900 B.C.
HT. $5\frac{1}{8}$ IN.
3B. ATTIC ('PROTOGEOMETRIC'). ABOUT 1000–900 B.C.
HT. $15\frac{5}{8}$ IN.
See page 23

4. ATTIC ('PROTOGEOMETRIC'). ABOUT 950–900 B.C.
HT. 14⅛ IN.
See page 23

5A. ATTIC ('GEOMETRIC'). 9TH CENTURY B.C. HT. $6\frac{5}{8}$ IN.
5B. ATTIC ('GEOMETRIC'). DETAIL FROM LARGE 8TH
CENTURY B.C. VASE
See pages 24, 25

6. ATTIC ('GEOMETRIC'). 8TH CENTURY B.C. HT 23⅝ IN.
See pages 24, 25

7A. ATTIC ('GEOMETRIC'). 8TH CENTURY B.C. HT. $9\frac{3}{4}$ IN.
7B. ATTIC ('GEOMETRIC'). 8TH CENTURY B.C. DIAM. $5\frac{6}{10}$ IN.
See pages 24, 25

8. ATTIC ('GEOMETRIC'). LATE 8TH CENTURY B.C.
See pages 24, 25

9. CYCLADIC (ISLAND OF THERA). EARLY 7TH CENTURY B.C.
HT. $25\frac{3}{4}$ IN.
See pages 24, 25

10A. 'PROTOCORINTHIAN'. EARLY 7TH CENTURY B.C. HT. $3\frac{1}{2}$ IN.
10B. 'PROTOCORINTHIAN'. FIRST HALF OF 8TH CENTURY B.C
HT. $8\frac{7}{8}$ IN.
See pages 26, 27

11A. 'PROTOCORINTHIAN'. EARLY 7TH CENTURY B.C. DIAM. 3 IN.
11B, C. FIRST HALF OF 8TH CENTURY B.C. HT. 9 AND $9\frac{1}{4}$ IN.
See pages 26–28

12A. 'PROTOCORINTHIAN'. SECOND QUARTER OF 7TH CENTURY B.C.
HT. $4\frac{7}{8}$ IN.
12B. RHODIAN. SECOND QUARTER OF 7TH CENTURY B.C.
See pages 26–28

13A, B. 'PROTOCORINTHIAN'. ABOUT 700 B.C.
13C. 'PROTO-ATTIC'. SECOND QUARTER OF 7TH CENTURY B.C.
See pages 26–28

14A. 'PROTO-ATTIC'. 700–675 B.C. DIAM. $10\frac{1}{4}$ IN.
See pages 26–28

15. CYCLADIC ISLANDS. FIRST HALF OF 7TH CENTURY B.C.
HT. 15¾ IN.
See pages 26–28

16A. RHODES. SECOND QUARTER OF 7TH CENTURY B.C. HT. $6\frac{3}{4}$ IN.
16B. RHODES. LAST QUARTER OF 7TH CENTURY B.C. DIAM. $14\frac{3}{4}$ IN.
See pages 29–31

17A. CHIOS. LATE 7TH CENTURY B.C. HT. $6\frac{1}{8}$ IN.
17B. CHIOS. LATE 7TH CENTURY B.C. DIAM. 15 IN.
See pages 29–31

18. RHODES. ABOUT 650–625 B.C. HT. $11\frac{1}{2}$ IN.
See pages 29–31

19A. EAST-GREEK. ABOUT 650–625 B.C. LENGTH $4\frac{3}{8}$ IN.
19B. CYPRUS. PERHAPS 7TH CENTURY B.C. HT. $8\frac{5}{8}$ IN.
See pages 29–31

20A. EAST-GREEK (PROBABLY RHODIAN). EARLY 6TH
CENTURY B.C. DIAM. 15 IN.
20B. EAST-GREEK (PROBABLY RHODIAN). EARLY 6TH
CENTURY B.C. DIAM. $11\frac{3}{8}$ IN.
See pages 29–31

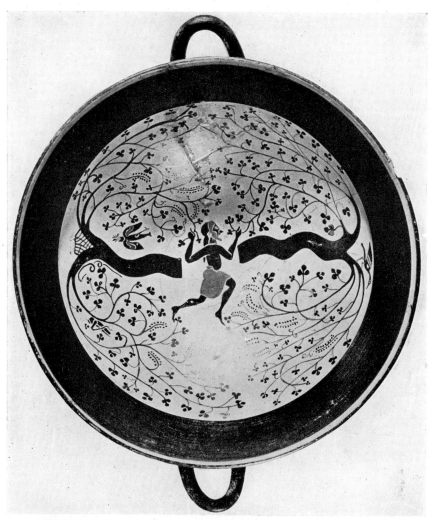

21A. EAST-GREEK. ABOUT 550 B.C. DIAM. $9\frac{3}{8}$ IN.
21B. EAST-GREEK. LATE 7TH CENTURY B.C. HT. $2\frac{1}{2}$ IN.
21C AND D. EAST-GREEK. FIRST HALF OF 6TH CENTURY B.C.
HT. $2\frac{3}{4}$ AND $3\frac{3}{4}$ IN.
See pages 29–31

22. CYCLADIC ISLANDS (PERHAPS PAROS). ABOUT 650 B.C.
HT. $20\frac{3}{4}$ IN.
See page 32

23A, B, D. 'PROTOCORINTHIAN'. ABOUT 675–650 B.C.
HT. $2\frac{1}{4}$, $2\frac{9}{16}$ AND $7\frac{1}{2}$ IN.
23C. 'PROTOCORINTHIAN'. ABOUT 640 B.C. HT. $2\frac{5}{8}$ IN.
See pages 33–35

24A. 'PROTOCORINTHIAN'. ABOUT 650–625 B.C. HT. 8¼ IN.
24B. 'PROTOCORINTHIAN'. DETAIL FROM JUG. ABOUT 640 B.C.
See pages 33–35

25A. 'PROTOCORINTHIAN'. ABOUT 640–625 B.C. HT. $7\frac{7}{8}$ IN.

25B, C. 'PROTOCORINTHIAN'. ABOUT 640–625 B.C. HT. $4\frac{15}{16}$ IN.

See pages 33–35

26A. 'PROTOCORINTHIAN'. ABOUT 650–625 B.C.
LENGTH $2\frac{9}{16}$ IN.
26B, C. CORINTHIAN ABOUT 600–570 B.C.
See pages 33–35

27A. 'PROTOCORINTHIAN' FRAGMENT. ABOUT 650 B.C.
27B. CORINTHIAN. ABOUT 570 B.C. DIAM. $7\frac{1}{2}$ IN.
See pages 33–35

28A. CORINTHIAN. ABOUT 600–575 B.C.
28B. CORINTHIAN. ABOUT 575–550 B.C. DIAM. $7\frac{1}{4}$ IN.
See pages 33–35

29. LAKONIAN. ABOUT 540 B.C. HT. 15½ IN.
See page 36

30A, B. LAKONIAN. TWO VIEWS OF SAME CUP. ABOUT 600 B.C.
See page 36

31A. LAKONIAN. ABOUT 550 B.C. DIAM. 8 IN.
31B. LAKONIAN. ABOUT 600–575 B.C. DIAM. 5$\frac{3}{8}$ IN.
See page 36

32. ATTIC BLACK-FIGURE. ABOUT 625–600 B.C. HT. $21\frac{1}{4}$ IN.
See pages 37, 38

55A. ATTIC BLACK-FIGURE. ABOUT 600–575 B.C. HT. $10\frac{1}{4}$ IN.
55B. ATTIC BLACK-FIGURE. ABOUT 600–575 B.C. HT. $6\frac{7}{8}$ IN.
See pages 37, 38

34. ATTIC BLACK-FIGURE. ABOUT 600–575 B.C. HT. 36$\frac{5}{8}$ IN.
See pages 37, 38

35A. ATTIC BLACK-FIGURE. ABOUT 580–575 B.C. DIAM. $8\frac{1}{4}$ IN.
35B. ATTIC BLACK-FIGURE. DETAIL FROM PLATE 34
See pages 37, 38

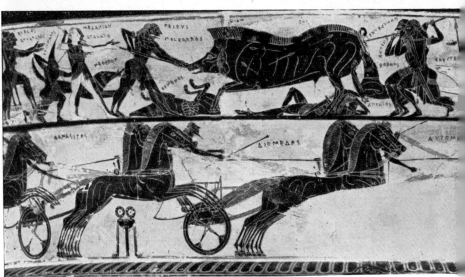

36A, B. ATTIC BLACK-FIGURE, THE 'FRANÇOIS VASE'
ABOUT 570–565 B.C. HT. 26 IN.
See pages 37, 38

37A, B. CORINTHIAN, WITH RED GROUND. ABOUT 575–550 B.C.
HT. 16¾ IN.
See pages 33–35

38A. ATTIC BLACK-FIGURE. ABOUT 575–550 B.C. DETAIL
INSIDE A CUP
38B. ATTIC BLACK-FIGURE. ABOUT 575–550 B.C. DIAM. 10½ IN.
See pages 37, 38

39A. ATTIC BLACK-FIGURE. ABOUT 550 B.C. DETAIL INSIDE
A CUP
39B. ATTIC BLACK-FIGURE. ABOUT 550 B.C. DIAM. $8\frac{1}{8}$ IN.
See pages 39, 40

40A, B. ATTIC BLACK-FIGURE. ABOUT 550–540 B.C.
DETAILS FROM CUPS LIKE PLATE 39B
40C, D. ATTIC BLACK-FIGURE. ABOUT 550–540 B.C.
DIAM. 8 IN.
See pages 39, 40

41A, B. ATTIC BLACK-FIGURE CUP, MADE BY EXEKIAS. ABOUT
540–530 B.C. DIAM. $11\frac{3}{4}$ IN.
See pages 39–41

42. ATTIC BLACK-FIGURE, MADE BY AMASIS. ABOUT 540 B.C.
HT. 12⅝ IN.
See pages 39–41

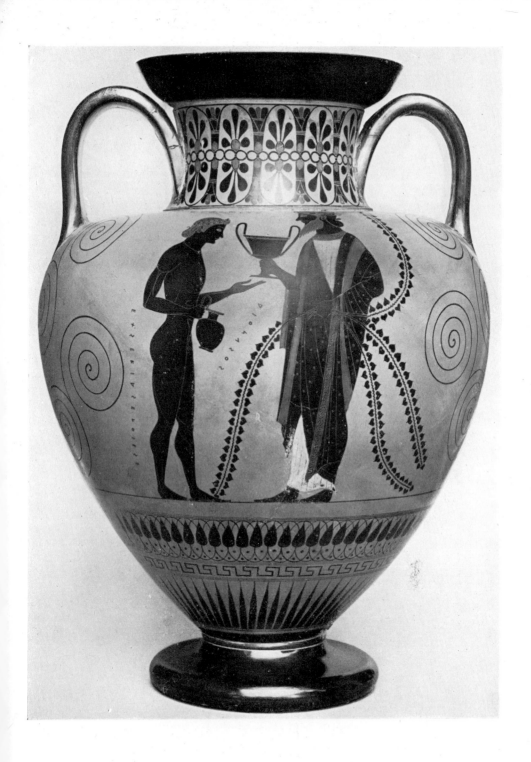

43. ATTIC BLACK-FIGURE, SIGNED BY EXEKIAS. ABOUT 540 B.C.
HT. $16\frac{3}{10}$ IN.
See pages 39–41

44. ATTIC BLACK-FIGURE, SIGNED BY EXEKIAS
ABOUT 540–530 B.C. HT. 31½ IN.
See pages 39–41

45A. ATTIC BLACK-FIGURE. FROM REVERSE
OF VASE ON PLATE 44
45B. ATTIC BLACK-FIGURE, SIGNED BY NEARCHOS. ABOUT 560 B.C.
See pages 39–41

46. ATTIC BLACK-FIGURE. ABOUT 520–500 B.C.
HT. $22\frac{7}{10}$ IN.
See pages 39–41

47. ATTIC BLACK-FIGURE. DETAIL FROM A VASE LIKE THAT
ON PLATE 46. ABOUT 520 B.C.
See pages 39–41

48. ATTIC BLACK-FIGURE. ABOUT 540–530 B.C.
See pages 39–41

49A. ATTIC BLACK-FIGURE. DETAIL FROM PLATE 48
49B. ATTIC BLACK-FIGURE. DETAIL FROM SIMILAR VASE
ABOUT 530–525 B.C.
See pages 39–41

50. ATTIC BLACK-FIGURE. ABOUT 500 B.C. HT. 24½ IN.
See pages 40, 41

51. ATTIC BLACK-FIGURE. ABOUT 500 B.C. HT. $29\frac{1}{2}$ IN.
See pages 40, 41

52A. ATTIC, BLACK-FIGURE. ABOUT 520 B.C. WITH WHITE
GROUND
52B. ATTIC BLACK-FIGURE. ABOUT 520 B.C. DIAM. $7\frac{1}{2}$ IN.
See pages 40, 41

53. ATTIC BLACK-FIGURE ON WHITE GROUND
ABOUT 520 B.C.
See pages 40, 41

54A. ATTIC BLACK-FIGURE. ABOUT 530–520 B.C. DIAM. 11 IN.
54B. 'CHALKIDIAN' BLACK-FIGURE. ABOUT 530 B.C.
DIAM. $15\frac{1}{4}$ IN.
See pages 40, 42

55A. ATTIC BLACK-FIGURE. ABOUT 540–520 B.C. HT. 5⅞ IN.
55B. 'CHALKIDIAN' BLACK-FIGURE. ABOUT 530 B.C.
See pages 40, 42

56. 'CHALKIDIAN' BLACK-FIGURE. ABOUT 540–530 B.C.
HT. 16$\frac{1}{8}$ IN.
See page 42

57. 'CHALKIDIAN' BLACK-FIGURE. ABOUT 540–530 B.C.
HT. $10\frac{1}{4}$ IN.
See page 42

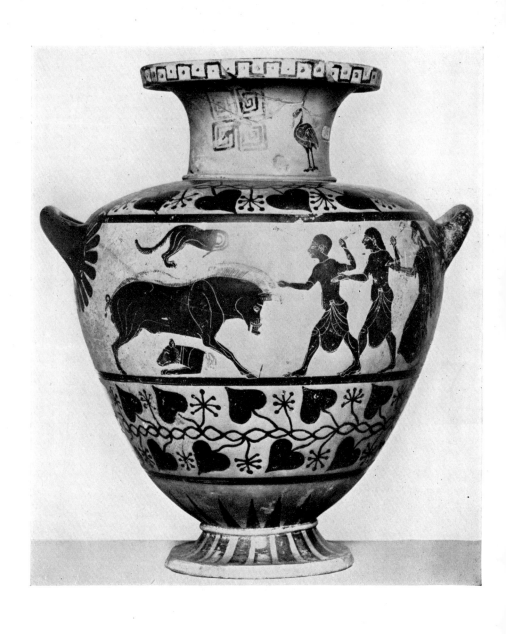

58. 'CAERETAN' BLACK-FIGURE. ABOUT 540–530 B.C.
HT. 17¼ IN.
See page 43

59. 'CAERETAN' BLACK-FIGURE. ABOUT 540–530 B.C.
HT. 17¾ IN.
See page 43

60A. EAST-GREEK. ABOUT 540 B.C. HT. 5¼ IN.
60B. DETAIL OF 'CAERETAN' VASE, LIKE PLATES 58, 59
ABOUT 540–530 B.C.
See page 43

61. EAST-GREEK OR ATTIC. ABOUT 540–530 B.C. HT. 10 IN.
See pages 43, 44

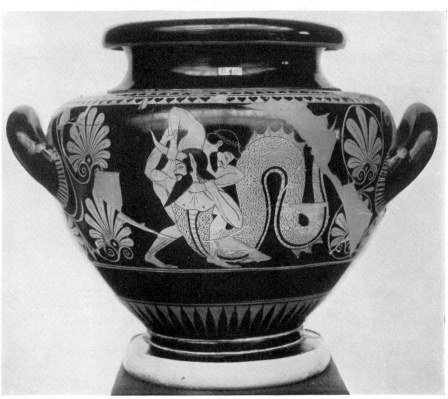

62A, B. ATTIC RED-FIGURE. ABOUT 525 B.C. HT. $10\frac{7}{8}$ IN.
See pages 45, 46

63A. ATTIC RED-FIGURE. ABOUT 530–520 B.C. HT. 5½ IN.
63B. ATTIC RED-FIGURE. ABOUT 530–520 B.C. DETAIL
FROM VASE LIKE PLATE 65
See pages 45, 46

64. ATTIC RED-FIGURE. ABOUT 525–520 B.C. HT. 14¾ IN.
See pages 45, 46

65. ATTIC RED-FIGURE. ABOUT 510–500 B.C. HT. $23\frac{5}{8}$ IN.
See pages 47–49

66A. ATTIC RED-FIGURE DETAILS. FROM PLATE 67
66B. ATTIC RED-FIGURE DETAILS. FROM PLATE 65
See pages 47–49

67. ATTIC RED-FIGURE. ABOUT 500–490 B.C. HT. $22\frac{1}{16}$ IN.
See pages 47–49

68A. ATTIC RED-FIGURE. ABOUT 500 B.C. HT. $13\frac{13}{16}$ IN.
68B. DETAIL FROM A SIMILAR VASE
See pages 47–49

69A, B. ATTIC RED-FIGURE. ABOUT 500–460 B.C. HT. $8\frac{1}{4}$ IN.
See pages 47–49

70A. ATTIC RED-FIGURE. ABOUT 520 B.C. DIAM. $7\frac{5}{8}$ IN.
70B. DETAIL FROM CUP LIKE COLOUR-PLATE C AND PLATE 75
ABOUT 510 B.C.
See pages 47–49

71A, B. ATTIC RED-FIGURE. DETAILS FROM INSIDE AND
OUTSIDE A CUP LIKE COLOUR-PLATE C AND PLATE 75
See pages 47–49

72A, B. ATTIC RED-FIGURE. ABOUT 510–500 B.C. DETAILS FROM
TWO CUPS LIKE COLOUR PLATE C AND PLATE 75
See pages 47–49

73A, B. ATTIC RED-FIGURE. DETAILS FROM A SINGLE CUP
LIKE COLOUR PLATE C AND PLATE 75
See pages 47–49

74A, B. ATTIC RED-FIGURE. ABOUT 490–480 B.C. SAME CUP
HT. $4\frac{7}{8}$ IN. DIAM. $10\frac{13}{16}$ IN.
See pages 47–50

75A, B. ATTIC RED-FIGURE. ABOUT 490–480 B.C. TWO
SIMILAR CUPS. DIAM. $12\frac{5}{16}$ IN. AND $12\frac{5}{8}$ IN.
See pages 48–50

76A. ATTIC RED-FIGURE. ABOUT 490–480 B.C. HT. $9\frac{1}{2}$ IN.
76B. ATTIC RED-FIGURE. ABOUT 470–465 B.C. LENGTH 6 IN.
See pages 48–50

77. ATTIC RED-FIGURE. ABOUT 480–470 B.C. HT. $11\frac{1}{4}$ IN.
See pages 48–50

78. ATTIC RED-FIGURE. ABOUT 480 B.C. HT. 25⅜ IN.
See pages 48–50

79. ATTIC RED-FIGURE. ABOUT 490–480 B.C. HT. $20\frac{3}{8}$ IN.
See pages 48–50

80. ATTIC RED-FIGURE. ABOUT 440 B.C. HT. $13\frac{1}{2}$ IN.
See pages 51, 52

81. ATTIC RED-FIGURE. ABOUT 470–460 B.C. HT. 15½ IN.
See pages 51, 52

82, 83A, B. ATTIC RED-FIGURE BELL-KRATER WITH DETAILS
BY THE PAN-PAINTER. ARTEMIS SLAYS ACTAEON
ABOUT 470–460 B.C. HT. 14¾ IN.
See pages 51, 52

84. ATTIC RED-FIGURE. ABOUT 470–460 B.C. HT. 14¾ IN.
See pages 51, 52

85. ATTIC RED-FIGURE. DETAIL OF AMPHORA. ABOUT 450 B.C.
See pages 51, 52

86. ATTIC RED-FIGURE. DETAIL OF AMPHORA
ABOUT 450 B.C.
See pages 51, 52

87. ATTIC RED-FIGURE. ABOUT 460–450 B.C. HT. $21\frac{1}{4}$ IN.
See pages 51, 52

88A. ATTIC VASE PAINTED IN COLOUR ON WHITE GROUND
ABOUT 475 B.C.
88B. ATTIC VASES PAINTED IN COLOUR ON WHITE GROUND. ABOUT
475–460 B.C. DIAM. OF GREATER $6\frac{5}{8}$ IN. HT. OF LESSER $3\frac{1}{4}$ IN.
See pages 53, 54

89A, B, C. ALABASTRA. 89D. KYLIX, PAINTED ON A WHITE
GROUND. ATTIC. ABOUT 500–480 B.C.
See pages 53, 54

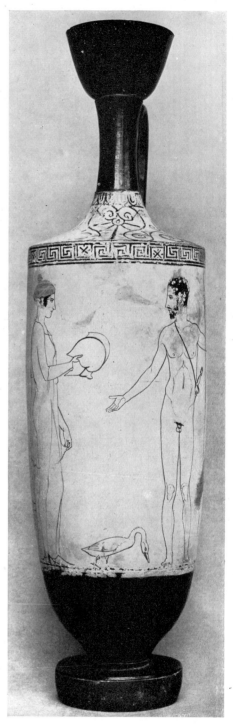

90A, B. ATTIC FUNERAL VASES PAINTED IN COLOUR ON WHITE
ABOUT 470 B.C. HT. 14 IN. AND 15½ IN.
See pages 53, 54

91A. ATTIC, PAINTED IN COLOUR ON WHITE. ABOUT 465 B.C.
HT. 6¾ IN.
91B. FLATTENED DETAIL FROM VASE LIKE PLATE 90B
See pages 53, 54

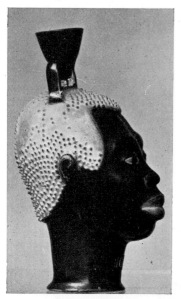

92A, B, C. ATTIC PLASTIC VASES. ABOUT 500–490 B.C.
HT. $5\frac{1}{2}$ IN., $7\frac{3}{8}$ IN. AND $8\frac{1}{4}$ IN.
See page 55

93A. 'TANAGRA' FIGURE, ONCE PAINTED IN COLOURS.
LATE 4th–3RD CENTURY B.C. HT. 9 IN.
93B. ATTIC RED-FIGURE. DETAIL OF TOILET BOX.
LATE 5TH CENTURY B.C.
See pages 55, 56, 57

94A. ATTIC RED-FIGURE. LATE 5TH CENTURY B.C. HT. $20\frac{1}{2}$ IN.
94B. ATTIC RED-FIGURE. LATE 5TH CENTURY B.C. DIAM. $2\frac{11}{16}$ IN.
See page 57

95A. BOEOTIAN CUP. 4TH CENTURY B.C. DIAM. $3\frac{1}{2}$ IN.
95B. 'MEGARIAN' BOWL. 3RD CENTURY B.C. DIAM. $4\frac{5}{8}$ IN.
See page 57

96. ATTIC HYDRIA. ABOUT 350 B.C. HT. $21\frac{1}{4}$ IN.
See pages 57, 58